New Life
for Men

New Life for Men

**A Book for Men
and the Women Who Care About Them**

Joe Vaughn & Ron Klug

AUGSBURG Publishing House • Minneapolis

NEW LIFE FOR MEN
A Book for Men and the Women Who Care about Them

Scripture quotations unless otherwise noted are from the Holy Bible: New International Version. Copyright 1978 by the New York International Bible Society. Used by permission of Zondervan Bible Publishers.

The quotation from Hugh Prather at the beginning of Chapter 7 is from *Notes to Myself* by Hugh Prather, copyright 1970 by Real People Press.

Library of Congress Cataloging in Publication Data

Vaughn, Joe, 1942-
    NEW LIFE FOR MEN.

    Bibliography: p. 155
    1. Men—Psychology. 2. Interpersonal relations.
3. Sex role. I. Klug, Ron. II. Title.
HQ1090.V38   1984   158'.088041   84-21685
ISBN 0-8066-2114-1 (pbk.)

Manufactured in the U.S.A.   APH 10-4642

1 2 3 4 5 6 7 8 9 0 1 2 3 4 5 6 7 8 9

To our wives and children,
companions on the journey.

Contents

Preface

- What does it mean to be a man today?
- How do we live and work with today's women?
- How can we find a healthy balance between our work, our family, and our own needs?
- How can we experience greater health and energy?
- How can we cope successfully with the stress and pressures of everyday life?
- How do we find meaning in a world where values are changing?

These are some of the questions many men are wrestling with today. This book is in part the record of our own struggles with these questions and some of the answers we have found for ourselves.

Joe Vaughn is 42 and a clinical psychologist in full-time practice in Rockford, Illinois. He works with children and adults and has counseled many men with both personal and family problems. He is married and the father of two daughters, one in college and one in junior high. His wife

Pat is a substitute teacher and is working toward a graduate degree in counseling.

Joe was raised on Chicago's northwest side and worked his way through college by driving a truck and waiting on tables. He has taught at the college level and is an active lay leader in the adult education program of his church. He enjoys running 5-10 miles a week, writing short stories, and fishing. He is a member of a men's support group that meets regularly in Rockford.

Ron Klug, age 44, has been a teacher, advertising copywriter, editor, and missionary. He grew up in a blue-collar family on the south side of Milwaukee. He supported himself through college by working on a landscape crew and as a dockworker. He is currently a free-lance writer and editor, working out of his home in Northfield, Minnesota. His wife Lyn teaches piano in their home and also writes. In his spare time Ron works out in an exercise group three times a week and is taking a karate class with his nine-year-old son. He sings in a church choir and teaches a Bible class. Every Tuesday morning he meets for breakfast with three other men who are in search of deeper friendships and mutual support.

In researching this book we also interviewed men that we felt were coping successfully with being a man in today's changing society. They represent a wide range of occupations, ages, and backgrounds. All the stories in this book are true, although at times names or details have been altered in order to protect confidentiality. When "Joe" or "Ron" are mentioned, these are always references to the authors.

Perhaps this book will speak especially to men who, like us, are in middle adulthood, married, and fathers. But we hope the book will also speak to younger men, singles, and divorced men.

If you are a woman reading this book, we hope it will help you gain a better understanding of issues facing today's men. We also hope that you might share this book with the men you care about.

We are of course aware that some men in our society are homosexual. Yet we have chosen not to deal with issues related to homosexuality because that is not our own orientation.

How to use this book

You may want to begin by just reading the book straight through. Chapters 1-3 lay a foundation for understanding ourselves in relationship to the changes happening in our society. Chapters 4-11 provide insights and practical techniques for improving the various aspects of our lives: feelings, friendships, work, leisure, marriage, family, and spiritual life. Chapter 12 will help you to determine what changes you might want to make in your life and aid you in setting priorities and goals.

Taking a close look at one's life and determining needed changes can be uncomfortable—or even painful. Sometimes we can be so overwhelmed by the need for changes that we feel like giving up. You may want to zero in on a few chapters that seem most important to you. Chapters 11 and 12 suggest some of the ways we receive strength to change.

To help you think through the issues raised by this book, we have included in each chapter some quizzes and self-testing exercises. We encourage you to use these as a way of applying what you read to your own life.

While you may read this book on your own, it will probably yield even more benefits if you discuss it with a group. The appendix suggests how to begin a men's support group, which might start by discussing this book.

Such a group is especially helpful if you decide you want to begin making some changes in your life. A second appendix provides some questions for discussion by a men's group. They could also be used by an individual who is trying to think through these issues in greater depth.

Whether you use this book alone or as part of a men's support group, we hope it will be an important resource for you on your personal journey toward new life.

1

Caught in the Middle

Every man is an exception.   *Søren Kierkegaard*

When their youngest child started first grade, Bill's wife wanted to finish her college degree. Although he wasn't sure why, Bill didn't like the idea. He preferred having her home. All she talked about were the people she was meeting at school and the new ideas she was encountering. Bill felt as if he were losing her.

Duane, a 48-year-old accountant, was always something of a loner. People thought of him as a nice guy, but quiet. He never had any problems with people at work or with his family, but then he never really seemed very happy, either. One night when his family was out, Duane committed suicide. Everyone wondered why. No one knew.

George, a 65-year-old restaurant owner, retired after working 12-14 hours a day for most of his adult life. Miserable and depressed, with no hobbies and "nothing to do," he died within six months of a massive heart attack.

Mike, an out-of-work auto mechanic, found himself relegated to the role of "househusband"—cooking, cleaning, and caring for two children while his wife worked full-time to support the family. After three months he sought counseling for sexual impotence and severe anxiety.

Fred, a middle-aged sales manager with international responsibilities, looked forward to slowing down and spending more time at home "one of these days." When he returned from a European business trip he discovered that his wife of 25 years had left him. He couldn't understand why.

These men are the typical casualties of our time. They represent millions of men facing a tangled web of interrelated problems:

- how to carve out a career in a rapidly changing economic scene
- how to maintain health in a society that offers too much food and drink and too little daily activity
- how to develop close personal relationships with both men and women
- how to adjust to the changing roles of women as they move toward greater equality
- how to deal with the crisis of retirement
- how to maintain harmonious family relationships
- how to find meaning and direction in a world where all values seem up for grabs

These issues challenge men who are accustomed to traditional male roles. The type of man that was needed to settle our frontier and power our industrial expansion is not the same type needed for our high-tech consumer- and service-oriented society. Beginning in the late 1960s the women's movement began to propel women into new roles, creating the potential for greater equality between the sexes. Male roles are undergoing radical change, and many men are caught in the middle of this transition.

Because our society is changing and women are changing, men will have to adapt in order to survive. Those who refuse to change will increasingly fall victim to high blood pressure, heart attacks, and other stress-related diseases. They will suffer from depression, emotional breakdowns, and other mental health problems. They will succumb to alcoholism and drug abuse. They will find themselves divorced from their wives and alienated from their children. And they will have no one to blame but themselves.

Men can change

None of this is necessary. Men *can* change. Men *need* to change—not just to be "nice guys," but fundamentally to survive. Those who choose to change will be healthier and live longer. They will be happier and get more enjoyment out of life. They will find more fulfillment in their life work.

In the process they will also become better husbands, friends, fathers, and members of their community.

In this book we have provided some basic information and practical techniques to enable men to move toward more positive and healthy ways of living in today's world.

If you read this book carefully, do the exercises, and begin to make some changes in your life, you will be better equipped to:

- be more aware of your feelings, accept them, and express them in helpful ways

- develop a variety of deeper and more satisfying relationships
- find a more healthy balance between work and leisure
- learn new ways to increase your health and energy
- find greater meaning in life and deepen your spiritual life
- develop a sense of direction for your life and set new goals and priorities

Where are you now?

In order to help you begin to think about the issues and questions raised in this book, we offer the following test. If you are a man, answer the questions for yourself. If you are a woman, answer the questions for a man in your life. You might both take the test and compare answers.

1. Do you engage in some form of regular, vigorous exercise at least twice weekly? ....Yes   No

2. Do you limit your consumption of alcohol to seven drinks or less per week? ....Yes   No

3. Did you refrain from smoking tobacco this week? ....Yes   No

4. Is your weight within 10 pounds of the average weight for your height?............................Yes   No

5. Did you initiate a social contact with a male friend in the past two weeks?....................................Yes   No

6. Are you part of a men's support group of some kind? ....Yes   No

7. Have you asked a friend for help or support in the past three months? ....Yes   No

8. Have you offered to help or support a friend in the past three months? ....Yes   No

9. Is it easy for you to talk about how you feel? ....Yes   No

10. In a sexual relationship do you give as much thought to your partner's needs and feelings as to your own?...Yes No

11. Have you done some housework this past week?
....Yes No

12. Were you the first person to apologize after your last argument? ....Yes No

13. Have you taken time to play with a child in the past two weeks? ....Yes No

14. Did you devote at least 20% of your time to your family last week?.......................................Yes No

15. Did you watch TV for less than seven hours last week?...Yes No

16. Have you expressed affection for someone in words or actions in the past 24 hours? ....Yes No

17. Have you complimented anyone on his or her performance at work this past week?.............Yes No

18. Have you taken a vacation or time off from your job in the past year?..Yes No

19. Have you been able to cry without feeling ashamed or guilty? ....Yes No

20. In the past week did you do something for your own spiritual growth?..Yes No

Scoring

Give yourself five points for each *yes* answer. Rate yourself according to the following scale, and then read on.

0-40   You're lost in the woods and need help fast!
45-60   You need to study the map and plan your life journey.
65-80   You're headed in the right direction, but need to make some corrections in your course.
85-100   You're an exceptional traveler, moving well on the journey to new life.

2

A Boy Becomes a Man

The child is the father of the man. *William Wadsworth*

Jerry Lindberg was born in the early 1950s, the first child in his family. His parents were pleased; they had wanted a boy first. His mother dressed him in blue, and his father bought him his first toy: a rubber football so big it barely fit in the crib. For his second birthday Jerry received a baseball glove; his third brought a gun-and-holster set. A tool kit, tricycle, Lincoln Logs, a chemistry set, and model airplanes followed.

When Jerry was eight, he came home from school in tears after being roughed up by the class bully. Mr. Lindberg told Jerry to "stop crying like a baby" and immediately took him out to buy boxing gloves. That night, and for several weeks after, Mr. Lindberg taught Jerry how to defend himself and to "fight like a man."

Jerry was encouraged, and even pressured, by both parents to excel in school. Mr. Lindberg wanted him to become a doctor, and often reminded him of the high grades he would need to enter medical school. Mrs. Lindberg thought it would be an honor to have Jerry graduate from college and be the kind of success that would make her feel proud.

Two more children were born into the family—both girls. As the children grew up, they all had responsibilities at home. Jerry's sisters did the dishes and helped with the cooking. Jerry took the garbage out and mowed the lawn. Both girls stayed close to home and were considerably more quiet than their brother. As the oldest and as a boy, Jerry was allowed to roam further, stay out later, and date earlier than his sisters. He also became more outspoken and more independent, and he was considered "all boy" by his family and neighbors.

Jerry played both football and baseball while he was in high school. His father encouraged him in sports and sometimes helped coach—when his work schedule allowed. On the weekends father and son watched sports on television. Often Jerry's mother prepared special meals and treats, assisted by her daughters, so that "the men" could have their food in front of the TV. Mrs. Lindberg was happy to encourage this behavior, because she felt that Mr. Lindberg did not spend enough time with Jerry.

Mr. Lindberg often worked overtime in the evenings and on weekends in order to provide the "extras" that he wanted for his family. This put a strain on his marriage and left little time for his family, but Mr. Lindberg felt it was necessary. He also drank on weekends, sometimes to excess. Mrs. Lindberg tried to explain this away by saying he needed to unwind, but she also resented his behavior. She didn't dare say anything openly to him, however, without risking a fight. Jerry and his sisters learned to stay out of their father's way when he was drinking.

Despite his father's shortcomings, Jerry admired him and tried to imitate his attitude and manner. Friends and family said Jerry was "a chip off the old block." They even smiled tolerantly when Jerry's temper flared and got him into trouble at school, a temper that reminded them of Mr. Lindberg.

Jerry went to college and graduated with a degree in business and accounting. Despite his father's mild disappointment at this career selection, Jerry justified it as "the best way to make big money."

Jerry married his college sweetheart, Sue. He liked her good looks, intelligence, and independent spirit. She was also a good cook, like his mother.

Following their wedding, Jerry started work at an excellent salary with one of the larger companies in the area. Within a few years he had several promotions, and by the time he was 26 he and his wife were able to buy a house in a fashionable suburb. Their first child—the son Jerry wanted—was born a year later, while Jerry was on an important business trip.

As Jerry climbed his personal career ladder, he found more and more need to retreat from the pressures and stress of his work, so he began to drink. After the birth of their second child, Jerry and Sue argued more frequently. Jerry began to spend even more time traveling for his job. On weekends he crashed in front of the TV or went out with the boys, leaving Sue to manage the kids.

Sue complained that Jerry acted like a spoiled little boy and that she had three children to take care of instead of two. She also accused Jerry of wanting sex on demand, with little regard for her feelings. Jerry seemed unwilling—or unable—to communicate with her about anything that mattered. She felt that he considered his job more important than his family and that he no longer loved her. At times she wondered if he ever had.

Sue started to read books concerned with women's issues and began to discuss these issues with friends. When she announced that she was taking a part-time job in order to use skills she had learned in college, Jerry was furious. The more she sensed that he was trying to control her life, the more she felt a need to break free of the relationship. She started going to church with the children in the hope of finding more meaning in her life. Jerry refused to go along because Sunday mornings were set aside for golf.

Jerry felt increasingly misunderstood by his wife and alienated from his children, who didn't seem to respect him the way he had respected *his* dad. At work he felt burned out. Although he had his drinking buddies, he didn't really have any good friends. Disillusioned and depressed at age 30, Jerry wondered what had gone wrong with his life.

How boys become men

The story of Jerry could be that of hundreds of thousands of American men. His story can help us understand some of the ways that boys learn what it means to be a man in our society. There are three primary influences on a man's early development: (1) the expectations and pressures of the society, (2) early learning experiences in the family, and later in school, and (3) the psychological process known as *identification*. Using Jerry's life as an example, let's look more closely at each of these influences.

1. Societal expectations and pressures

Men are in trouble today, in part because of societal

and cultural expectations. Middle-class American males traditionally have been encouraged to be active, aggressive, independent, competitive, and achievement-oriented. To some extent, these are valuable traits, especially in a success-oriented, competitive society. At first these traits served Jerry quite well. He fit into the system and found success in school and in his career. Jerry knew how to move up the corporate ladder and compete aggressively in the marketplace. Yet he had not learned nearly as well how to work cooperatively or relate sensitively to the needs and feelings of others. It was especially hard for him to relate to women as equal partners.

2. *Early family experiences*

The process by which early experiences shape masculine identity begins almost at birth. In Jerry's life, even his toys were representative of the sex-role identity that was expected. The pattern was established early by a father and mother who valued sons over daughters and who saw rigid and prescribed roles for each.

Jerry's early family experiences reinforced society's expectations for boys and men. Jerry's father was, in all ways, a traditional male, and he transmitted traditional male values to Jerry by teaching him to defend himself, to compete with others, and to focus on his own needs, goals, and objectives. Because they had no other perspective, Jerry's mother and sisters supported this, and Jerry learned to expect certain rights and privileges associated with being male. While this caused little difficulty in a family that had accepted these roles and expectations, it became a problem 20 years later in Jerry's own marriage. Society was changing, and Jerry was married to a woman who had begun to press for the satisfaction of some of her own needs as an equal partner in the relationship.

3. *The process of identification*

Identification has been called the most powerful psychological process in the formation of sex-role behavior. The identification process involves more than a young boy observing and imitating his father's behavior. It is a boy's acting as if he were similar to his father, possessing his father's thoughts, feelings, and characteristics. Identification with his father was Jerry's way of creating closeness with his parent. There was security in feeling like his father—powerful, confident, and in control.

The identification process, however, requires some emotional connection with a role model. Identification happens when a parent possesses qualities that are attractive to a child and when the child sees himself or herself as similar to the parent. A child identifies most readily with a parent who is seen as competent and caring, rather than weak or rejecting.

Identification can be a valuable process. A child who identifies with a healthy, effective parent can gain confidence and learn important skills for life. But in the identification process, the child often picks up the parent's weaknesses and problems. This may cause difficulties in later life.

Jerry identified with a father who was loving, hardworking, and relatively stable, who took care of his family's material needs in a responsible manner. However, he also identified with a father who overworked at the expense of his wife and children, used alcohol to manage stress, and vented his anger in outbursts of temper and aggressive behavior.

Jerry arrived at a crisis point in his life in part because of the influences, expectations and experiences that molded him as a man. Many men are at a similar point or in the midst of other conflicts associated with the ways they were taught to be men, ways that no longer work as well in our changing society.

Like Jerry, many men have problems establishing and maintaining close personal relationships because they have not learned how to do it. They may not have observed it in their fathers, and society may not encourage it. Without an adequate model for developing close relationships or the encouragement to develop them, these are not established. And because they are not established, they are not demonstrated or taught to the next generation. Thus a barren, destructive cycle is perpetuated.

The changing scene

Many, perhaps most of the men reading this book have, like the authors, grown up with a traditional understanding of what it means to be a man. We have probably learned to accept a list of stereotyped traits like these:

Masculine	*Feminine*
tough	tender
independent	dependent
logical	emotional
assertive	passive
strong	weak
silent	talkative
brave	fearful
competitive	cooperative
cool	warm
firm	gentle

Some of the traits we have learned as "masculine" are valuable. They help us live effective, successful, meaningful lives. Some traditionally "masculine" traits are life-enhancing. But others are neither valuable nor life-enhancing. Still others are just plain destructive. We pursue them at great cost to our own health and happiness.

The good news is that we can change. Even though we have been programmed to accept certain life patterns as being masculine, we can modify the program. In fact, because society is changing and women are changing, men today need to make certain changes simply for the sake of survival, as well as for the sake of others. Here is a way to begin:

1. We can become more aware of the traditional masculine/feminine stereotypes and the extent to which we have accepted them.

2. We can realize that these traditional stereotypes are not all based on biological differences. They are not necessarily "natural"; not all have been decreed by God. (In fact, as we will see later, our religious heritage has some insights that may help us out of our present dilemma.) Many of these so-called masculine traits are simply a part of our culture.

3. We can be open to change—to retain what is healthful in our concept of masculinity and change what is destructive. In the past 25 years the women's movement has helped many women rethink what it means to be a woman. In the process many have found greater happiness and personal success. We men need a new awareness that will help us identify attitudes and habits that cripple us and discover those that enable us to live more fully and effectively.

The new journeyman

Our generation of men is caught living "between the times." Like Jerry, most of us have inherited certain ideas of masculinity and male behavior. Some of these we may be aware of; others we may not be. In recent years many men have become more aware of the destructiveness of these "macho" patterns and are choosing new ways of thinking and acting.

The trouble for many of us is that while we had strong role models for the traditional way of being a man (fathers, uncles, older brothers), we have few models for the new way. We are in some sense pioneers on a new frontier of masculinity.

While there may not be many role models for the new way, there are men who are finding new ways that are more healthful and life-giving. We have chosen to call these *journeymen*. This is a term rich with historical associations in the lives of working men. The word *journeyman* suggests a man who has knowledge and skills, yet is open to learning new ways based on experience. A journeyman has moved beyond the apprentice or beginner stage, but is not yet a master craftsman. He is on a journey to find a new way of life.

The men we call *journeymen* are no longer imprisoned by rigid notions of how males are supposed to behave or respond. Instead they are exploring new and creative solutions to situations and challenges in their day-to-day living.

In his fascinating book *Blue Highways: A Journey into America*, William Least Heat Moon describes the importance of the exploration process when he writes: "Any traveler who misses the journey misses about all he's going to get—that a person becomes his attentions, they make and remake him." By contrast the novice traveler sees value only in how many miles of interstate are logged each day. Blindly destination-bound, such a traveler sees interruptions only as delays, and considers exploration a waste of time.

A journeyman is willing to leave the interstate of a driven, nonthinking, unfeeling life-style and explore the "blue highways" in his life, paying attention to the process of his own travel. He has learned that interruptions may be an important part of life because they help us focus on the here and now of our lives rather than on the past or the future. He appreciates the truth that "life is what happens while we're busy making other plans." In short, a journeyman is living on the growing edge of his life.

The remaining chapters of this book will help you develop your own life-direction as a man in today's society. But to give you some encouragement right now about the potential for change, here are some examples of men we have chosen to call journeymen:

Bill, a 40-year-old psychiatrist, voluntarily reduced the time he spent in his own thriving practice to take care of his three children while his wife returned to college to earn the diploma she sacrificed for his medical training.

Bob, a highly successful businessman, had a strong religious experience that led him to reexamine the purpose of his life. Although he had teenage children, he began college studies and later enrolled in a seminary. On his graduation he became an overseas missionary.

Wayne, the single father of two preschool daughters, cooks meals, washes clothes, and cleans house while running his business from his home so that the girls' care does not have to be entrusted to a day-care center.

Steve, age 50, has put together a job package that includes teaching English half-time at a local college, free-lance writing, and helping his wife with her work as a commercial artist. In his spare time you might find him covered with grease from tearing an engine apart or sitting quietly in his study writing a poem.

A sales manager in his late 50s, Keith decided to take early retirement to explore some other possibilities for his life. He wound up devoting his full-time effort to volunteer service in his community.

3

The Journey Inward

The journey inward is the longest journey.
Dag Hammarskjöld

Like Jerry Lindberg, each of us has traveled the journey from boyhood to adult manhood. As writers like Daniel Levinson and Gail Sheehy have shown, there are some predictable stages and crises that men pass through on their journey in life. But there is another kind of journey that men—and women—need to make: the journey inward.

The journey inward is a very threatening experience for a man. This territory is highly personal and almost always uncharted. It involves looking inside oneself, examining feelings, fears, strengths, and weaknesses. It means having to face ourselves and assess our values, our beliefs, and our attitudes with the knowledge that we might be found lacking. In short, looking within means taking the risk of being vulnerable in the hope of achieving personal growth.

There are several reasons why many men hesitate on the threshold of such a journey. Because they have tended to focus on action and achievement rather than feelings and inner experiences, many men are reluctant to look within themselves and try to make sense out of what they find there. Paying attention to emotions and feelings may constitute a threat to their masculinity. And because this journey involves a good deal of conscious choice on the part of the traveler, it is easy for some men simply to refuse to make the trip.

Although a man can begin this inner journey at any time in his adult life, there are some indications that this personal pilgrimage is most likely to occur during middle adulthood. Carl Jung points out that the first half of a man's life is concerned with achievement and building a career. Jung also maintains that the second half of life is when the inner self is most likely to develop. He cautions that if this inner self does not find expression, the individual will encounter problems because the needs and requirements of the second half of life are very different from those of the first half.

The journey inward may also be triggered by important situations and events. These are often disruptive, and even traumatic, experiences that force us to look at ourselves, our behavior, and our lives in new and different ways. While this can be a frightening prospect, it also holds great potential. In the example in Chapter 2, Jerry's career and marriage had to begin coming apart at the seams before he realized that the way he was handling his life was not working. Divorce, serious illness, unemployment, a career change, the death of a close friend or loved one—each of these carries the seeds of change and even personal growth, if we can open ourselves to what they may have to teach us.

But how much do we know of the specifics of this inner journey? Are there any maps to follow? What kind of changes do men in our society need to make? And what are some of the issues involved? The answers to these questions are far from clear, but the following chart suggests some of the terrain that today's men need to explore.

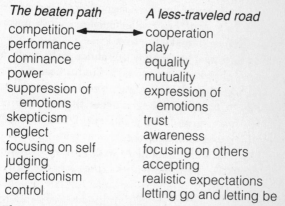

The beaten path	A less-traveled road
competition ←→	cooperation
performance	play
dominance	equality
power	mutuality
suppression of emotions	expression of emotions
skepticism	trust
neglect	awareness
focusing on self	focusing on others
judging	accepting
perfectionism	realistic expectations
control	letting go and letting be

The two columns represent two ways of living. Both are possible alternatives at various times and stages in a man's life. Ideally, we learn how to move between these two poles, blending them into a personal path unique to ourselves and our life situation. Problems occur when a man adopts a rigid, unthinking, all-or-nothing commitment to one pole or the other.

As we have seen, men in our society are more likely to get stuck on what we have identified as the "beaten path." This heavily traveled life pattern has been reinforced by cultural and early parental influences and by the accompanying illusion of control and individual success. Despite some of the benefits it provides, exclusive adherence to this path over a long period can send a man on a lifetime journey of interpersonal conflict, distance from others, and emotional barrenness.

Alternatives *do exist* to this "beaten path." A man has the opportunity to explore a "less traveled" and more flexible road. While this may be an unfamiliar journey for many men, it can lead to greater personal awareness, a broader perspective about the world, and more meaningful and effective relationships with others. The choosing of one's inner "path" is not a one-time, all-or-nothing choice. Rather, the selection process is continuous. A man needs to be able to move back and forth between the two poles, choosing actions and attitudes that are most workable for his own life.

For now we will be content to describe briefly each polarity. In succeeding chapters we will see how traveling down these different paths might affect some of the major areas of a man's life, including work, marriage, family, physical health, leisure time, and spiritual growth.

Competition—cooperation

Our society rewards competitive attitudes and behavior. This is especially true of the business community and the world of sports, where "winning" often leads to success. However, cooperation and working together are far more effective in personal relationships, marriage, and the family. Too many men are unable to switch gears from competing to cooperating, and so experience considerable conflict with others.

Steve reports, "In school I was a really tough competitor in basketball. As a result I had a real temper. Most of the time I was mad at myself. Finally one day I got tired of it. I said to myself, '*Enough of that. Today I'm just going to go out there and have fun.*' It worked. Even my teammates noticed it. From then on I enjoyed basketball a lot more, and I carried that attitude over into other areas of my life. Now when things don't go my way at work, I can accept that. I don't have to win 'em all."

Performance—play

In a man's world performance, achievement, and ambition are highly valued. But unceasing travel along this path may reduce a man's ability to experience the release and refreshment that comes through play and spontaneous enjoyment. A life that is all performance and no play increases the risk of stress-related problems and illness. A balance between meaningful work, personal accomplishment, and a healthy use of leisure time is important in a man's life.

Dominance—equality

Dominance implies ruling over and running over others. Dominating the product market in the business world or ruling the NFL standings are the types of goals many men have. But the skills and attitudes men use to pursue these goals do not necessarily transfer to situations in which relationships with others are paramount. The sharing of rights and privileges is an important part of getting along with others. Partnership and equality are what make friendships and marriages work.

Power—mutuality

Power can be used appropriately and for the benefit of others. But it is also true that power corrupts. The excessive and inappropriate control of people or things may destroy a man's capacity for close relationships. Power needs to be balanced by mutuality, by sharing with others. The kind of give-and-take required in healthy human relationships cannot happen if a man operates only from a stance of power and domination.

Suppression of emotions—expression of emotions

The expression of feelings is a problem for most men. Although it is not necessary or even healthy for all emotions to be expressed at all times, men can work toward more balance. As we will see in Chapter 4, the denial and suppression of feelings can lead to serious physical and emotional problems.

Ted, a 36-year-old lawyer, tells how he was able to express powerful feelings at a crisis in his life: "The first time I took my bar exams, the results were due to come while I was on vacation in Upper Michigan. When we got there I had to walk about a hundred yards to use somebody's phone. I called to see how I did on the exams and learned that I had failed. I just about died. I started crying—inside. I had to walk all the way back. I felt like a little kid. I curled up in our camper and started to cry. My wife came over and curled up next to me. She held me and finally I went to sleep."

Skepticism—trust

The ability and willingness to trust in other people and in some meaning and purpose beyond ourselves is essential if we are to grow. Unfortunately, many men pride themselves on their skepticism and doubt toward anything or anyone other than themselves. "I'll believe it when I see it" or "The only person you can trust is yourself" are familiar mottoes that diminish a man's ability to trust.

Neglect—awareness

Despite our society's increased awareness about the

importance of physical health and emotional well-being, too many men continue down the path of neglect for their own bodies and minds. We need to learn to take care of ourselves in ways that value and conserve our God-given gifts.

At age 42 Stan was aware that he had put on about 30 extra pounds, mostly hanging over his belt. When he started having trouble sleeping at night, he decided to take some action. "I realized I was taking too much tension home from work with me. I took advantage of an introductory offer at a health club in the neighborhood. Now I go in for a good strenuous workout at least three evenings a week. I'm sleeping much better, and I'm getting my weight down to where it belongs."

Focusing on self—focusing on others

The man who is self-focused is self-reliant and self-concerned. While these characteristics are a necessary part of being an adult, carried to an extreme they prevent men from considering the needs of others. Joe reports: "I find myself much more concerned about other people now. I think I'm a better father and a better husband because of it. My main focus used to be my own accomplishment—finishing my degree, moving up in my career. My father's message to me always was: 'Be the best. Be number one.' I did perform and compete, and I was rewarded for it. But when you're caught up in performing, you don't have much time for anything else. Now I try to take more time with my wife and family and for myself. I still have to remind myself to do it, though. It's so easy to get caught up in the *shoulds* and *oughts* rather than in the *wishes* and *wants*."

On the other end of the continuum are men, particularly in the helping professions like medicine or the ministry, who are so busy caring for others that they neglect their own needs. At some point in our lives all of us need to feel we can depend on the love and care of others. We need to learn how to receive care as well as give it. A good friend once told Ron, "You know, you really need to let people do something *for you* sometimes. You need it, and so do they."

Judging—accepting

A traditional man, treading the beaten path, is often hard on other people and on himself. He expects the best and is quick to pounce on faults or shortcomings in his spouse, children, or colleagues. While this is another characteristic that can lead to success, it can also be destructive to others, especially when carried to extremes. A more healthy attitude is acceptance of others for who they are and the giving of support and encouragement rather than faultfinding and criticism.

Perfectionism—realistic expectations

Closely related to judging and accepting is the dichotomy between striving for ultimate perfection in everything we do and being satisfied with good performance. Paradoxically, trying too hard can sometimes prevent the success that we strive for so diligently. Sometimes the way to improve your golf game is to relax and quit trying so hard. In writing, too, the striving for perfection can lead to a cumbersome style. The good writer knows how to let go and let the writing happen.

Control—letting go and letting be

A critical challenge for most men is to be able, when necessary, to make the transition from directing, managing, and taking charge to allowing things and people to be as they are. We call this "letting go and letting be."

This control issue undergirds most of the dichotomies on the inner journey map. The traditional male role values control: over the *world* (ambition, achievement, and performance); over *others* (competition, dominance, and power); and over *self* (inhibition and denial of feelings, independence and self-reliance).

When we "over-control," as many men are prone to do, we take too much on ourselves. We become worn down and feel burdened by worries, problems, and concerns. We feel we are personally responsible for solving things. Men would benefit greatly from the ability to move to a more relaxed and noncontrolling state. The man who is unable to explore the less traveled road of letting go and letting be risks a variety of male diseases including ulcers, workaholism, high blood pressure, cardiovascular problems, and early death.

While achievement and independence are certainly important, a man also needs to balance these with the ability simply to accept who he is and to enjoy things as they are. When he can do this, he gains a healthier perspective on his life and can return to his responsibilities refreshed and revitalized.

The key is flexibility

Most men are more accustomed to the beaten path than to the less-traveled road. But we are not saying that one of these is bad and the other good. If either one is carried to an extreme or followed exclusively, a man's chances for happiness and success are reduced.

The real key is flexibility—being able to move back and forth between the two poles, choosing the strategy that works best in a given situation.

Where do you fit in right now? Rank yourself on the scale that follows each of the dichotomies listed below, based on where you *usually* are—which path you follow most often and to what extent. (You may need to indicate an "average" because you act one way at work and another way at home. But try to indicate where you think you fit at this point in your life.)

competition							cooperation		
1	2	3	4	5	6	7	8	9	10

performance							play		
1	2	3	4	5	6	7	8	9	10

dominance							equality		
1	2	3	4	5	6	7	8	9	10

power							mutuality		
1	2	3	4	5	6	7	8	9	10

suppression of emotions							expression of emotions		
1	2	3	4	5	6	7	8	9	10

skepticism							trust		
1	2	3	4	5	6	7	8	9	10

neglect							awareness		
1	2	3	4	5	6	7	8	9	10

focusing on self							focusing on others		
1	2	3	4	5	6	7	8	9	10

judging							accepting		
1	2	3	4	5	6	7	8	9	10

perfectionism							realistic expectations		
1	2	3	4	5	6	7	8	9	10

control							letting go and letting be		
1	2	3	4	5	6	7	8	9	10

4

Men Have Feelings Too

There is a time for everything, and a season for every
activity under heaven . . . a time to weep and a time to
laugh, a time to mourn and a time to dance . . . .
Ecclesiastes 3:1, 4

As we have seen, the beaten path for men is a way of
life dominated by an excessive need to control oneself,
one's environment, and others. This path also involves
the suppression of feelings rather than their expression.
From early on, most men have learned to suppress and
deny their emotions, having been taught directly and indirectly that feelings are at best an unnecessary nuisance
and at worst an indication of weakness and male inadequacy.

To have strong feelings and to express them openly is
in direct contradiction to the masculine characteristics
valued by our culture. The male emphasis on independence and assertiveness does not encourage the admis-
sion of inadequacy, fear, or personal uncertainty.

Here again, it is necessary to point out that typically "masculine" traits like competitiveness, self-reliance, and toughness are not wrong or bad. They become harmful only when they are pursued to the exclusion of others that are also valuable. A one-sided focus on these traditionally male characteristics blocks the growth of equally desirable traits, especially those that are necessary if a man is to have access to the full range of his feelings and emotions.

Understanding the nature of feelings

Several points need to be made about feelings:

Feelings can cause difficulty when they are mixed.   It is normal to feel more than one thing at a time. It is rare, for example, that a person simply feels depressed. Guilt, inadequacy, self-hate, and even anger are also usually a part of the picture. Try to recall your high school or college graduation or your wedding day. Chances are you won't be able to completely define any one of those important events in your life in terms of a single feeling.

When feelings are mixed, the problem becomes one of sorting out what's there. To do that we have to pay attention to our emotional state. While it isn't easy for a man to get used to "consulting" his feelings, the result can be important personal growth.

Feelings can cause difficulties when they are in conflict.   A man worried about growing old might feel both proud of and threatened by a son who is a successful athlete. Or following an upsetting argument with his wife, a husband could feel quite guilty and uncomfortable and wish to apologize to her while still harboring a great deal of anger and resentment toward her for something she may have said in the heat of her own anger. Such clearly contradictory feelings directed toward someone we love are likely to be confusing and disturbing. When our feelings present us with this kind of internal conflict, it may seem easiest at the time not to think about them at all. However, we will see that following this path can lead to serious problems.

Feelings are closely related to our thinking. Feelings don't just happen, they are caused. But caused by what? The most common answer has been, "Why, other people of course, and the situations and events we encounter in our lives." But the truth is that we actually create our *own* emotions and feelings based on *how and what we think* about those other people and the situations we encounter. Even when a genuinely negative event occurs in our lives, it is the meaning we attach to that event or to the persons contributing to that event that determines our emotional response.

It is natural to believe that external events cause our feelings. But if we can accept the fact that we are responsible for our own feelings, we will have the opportunity to take charge of how we feel. We can never completely control what happens to us. But when we can accept the fact that we are telling ourselves how to feel, we are then better able to do something about those feelings.

Feelings cannot be controlled by suppressing, ignoring, or repressing them. The more one attempts to ignore or deny feelings, the more one loses control over them. What many men fail to understand is that when feelings are held in, they may build to a point where one has little or no ability to evaluate them or gauge their intensity. It is then that the emotions control the man.

It has been said that not feeling anything is the worst feeling of all. Unfortunately, the absence of feelings is a condition from which many men suffer. How is it possible not to have any feelings? Psychologists have offered several explanations.

Suppression or the conscious holding back and holding in of feelings is a common way in which men attempt to master and control their emotions. Many men have learned this technique from fathers who were unable to manage their feelings or who openly criticized the expression of any emotion. A friend reports that when his father would see men on television expressing strong emotions, he would snort, "Look at that fairy!" That father was clearly unable to cope with his own feelings or those of his family. Just as important, however, was the negative lesson he taught his son: "Men who display feelings openly are fairies."

Where suppression is operating to a significant degree, another process is often at work, a psychological defense mechanism called *repression*. This process involves the actual unconscious "forgetting" or denial of thoughts and feelings that are frightening or upsetting. When thoughts and emotions are too painful to be experienced or remembered at all, they are packed away outside the conscious mind. The result is both good and bad for the person. On the positive side, when these thoughts and feelings are unconscious they are not around to threaten one's personal equilibrium. More negatively, thoughts and feelings in their unconscious form never go very far away. They continue to affect the person's behavior and mood indirectly, causing difficulties in the form of inconsistent and sometimes unpredictable behavior or vague uneasiness, tension, and anxiety.

In talking with a number of men, we discovered that

the feelings that seemed to trouble them most were anger, sexual attraction to other women, and fear— particularly fear of failure. It isn't easy for any man to deal openly and directly with feelings like these, but more men are accepting the "humanness" of such emotions. Too often, however, the typical male response is to try to avoid or deny them or to stuff them back inside where they came from. The prevailing attitude seems to be, "If I don't let anyone (including myself) know I feel this way, I'll be able to control myself better." Nothing could be further from the truth.

Men have different reasons for denying feelings. Many do so because they are actually operating from a position of weakness rather than strength. Those who are threatened by their own strong feelings of inadequacy and personal insecurity have a desperate need to deny feelings, because these emotions seem to prove the already negative judgment they have handed down on their own masculinity. To admit to having feelings would be to acknowledge that they are not "real men."

A man who uses excessive denial to handle feelings may try to present himself as always being in charge. Such a person will like to dominate conversations, brag about his successes, and maintain the fiction that he has no weaknesses. Unfortunately, this kind of man often does not make a good husband or father (except for providing material things, a task at which he is often quite good!). In a crisis he is frequently "not there" physically or emotionally. He is surprised when people are upset and can't understand why it's necessary to get "all worked up over nothing." He can't allow himself to recognize or express his emotions about anything because that would be too threatening to his personal integrity.

Whatever the reason for not expressing feelings, the

result is almost always trouble. Here are some of the unfortunate possibilities.

Unexpressed feelings

Unexpressed feelings are often released in an explosive or unpredictable manner.   A respected businessman and community leader, John was rumored to be a future candidate for Congress. People marveled at his coolness under pressure. Despite heavy stress levels associated with both his business and his public service, he was calm and collected. He seemed in complete control at all times. He went out of his way to help friends and acquaintances and never showed anger.

His family, however, saw a different side of him. Around the house he was often moody and irritable. One Sunday the lawnmower wouldn't start. In a fit of rage, John threw a wrench through the windshield of his wife's car. When she complained, he lost control and began to hit her. The police were called, and the story made the local papers. John's marriage was thrown into turmoil, and his political career was over.

Unexpressed feelings can cause physical problems and complications.   Although he was only 38, Henry already had a history of chronic neck, back, and leg pain which he attributed to an "arthritic condition" suffered by several in his family. His pain was so disruptive that it caused him to miss work and prevented him from being able to lie down for extended periods. When his internist began to observe a connection between the intensity of Henry's pain and the degree of stress in his family relationships, he referred him for psychological evaluation.

The psychologist found that Henry harbored longstanding feelings of anger and resentment toward both his mother and his wife. Without an ability to understand or appropriately handle and express these feelings, Henry had developed "chronic pain syndrome." Marital counseling, rather than additional pain-control medication, was recommended, and it proved effective in reducing the crippling effects of Henry's pain.

Unexpressed feelings reduce the capacity for close relationships and separate us from others. The Johnsons surprised most of their relatives and all of their neighbors when their marriage of 15 years ended in divorce. In couples therapy, Mrs. Johnson revealed her frustrations with a husband who never missed a day of work but never remembered her birthday or their anniversary. She complained bitterly about a man who refused to discuss their relationship problems and who would only talk of current events and the most routine matters. Discussion about family and friends he called "gossip," and the expression of feelings he labeled "nonsense." The last straw had been Mr. Johnson's suggestion that they limit their sexual relationship to once a month or so because of the "bother" it caused.

Unexpressed feelings make it difficult for a man to acknowledge his own needs and to ask for help when necessary. A young optometrist, just beginning his own practice, attempted suicide in his office by cutting his wrists. His partner found him in time and he was rushed to the emergency room of the local hospital. In the treatment that followed, it was discovered that his depression was associated with strong feelings of professional inadequacy and an intense fear of failure. His wife denied any awareness of his depression, saying that he had complained only of "tiredness." His partner, who had attended optometry school with him, said he could not remember a time when his friend had even hinted at any doubts about himself or his capabilities.

Unexpressed feelings create emotional problems and difficulties.   A high school science teacher who did not understand or acknowledge the degree of his own anger toward young people developed a phobia that involved his inability to teach without the classroom door propped open. A repetitive dream in which he attacked his infant son provided the key to unlocking long-suppressed feelings of anger and resentment.

Managing feelings in a healthier way

A man's inner journey is not complete unless it includes an encounter with his own feelings. This part of the journey within is difficult for most men because for so long their lives have been ruled by their heads rather than their hearts. In a man's world, feelings have been a handicap. They have gotten in the way. Unlike facts and figures, plans and goals, feelings and emotions are harder to take hold of. They are imprecise and often irrational. While it's true that feelings complicate our lives and our relationships with others, they also provide much of the substance and spice of our existence.

Some men have been willing to put up with the awkwardness and uncertainty that accompanies getting to know one's feelings better. In the process they have discovered that they can enjoy life more fully and be more effective in managing their emotions. As they respond to their feelings, they are able to see them in a new way. They learn how to change them or put them to better use. In today's "computerese," feelings that are experienced, understood, and expressed are feelings that become "user friendly."

One middle-aged man, raised in a home with a "traditional" father, talked about his path to a better way of handling his feelings.

I saw my father as very "manly," very "masculine," and as a man who did not show a lot of affection toward other men. He was a "man's man." I think for a long time in my life I tried to put my feelings in the background too—or at least not let them show. Now I'm trying to be very aware of why I'm feeling the way I am. An example is if I'm upset with a person at work, I try to focus on why I'm upset with that person. Instead of just getting mad at the person for being like that, I try to look at both sides and own up to the fact that the person is who he is and what he is and I have to go about finding out what is really upsetting me.

David sought counseling after a vocational crisis and the breakup of his marriage. He said, "When the counselor first talked about feelings, my reaction was, 'I don't have any feelings.' My feelings were so buried that I didn't know I had any. Gradually I became more aware of them and learned to talk about them."

How to express feelings

Okay, so you learn that it's all right to have feelings and you're encouraged to express those feelings. But how do you start to do that in ways that seem natural for you and that don't hurt other people? Here are some suggestions:

1. Pay attention to what you are feeling and thinking. Try to identify what it is—hurt, anger, depression, or confusion—and then see if you can figure out what caused the feeling. What are you telling yourself in the way of thoughts, beliefs, and misbeliefs that may be creating your feeling?

Joe says: "Handling feelings of anger still gives me some trouble. Learning how to talk them out has helped, but of most value for me has been paying attention to the thoughts behind the feelings. I've been most successful at managing anger when I've been able to identify what I'm thinking about the person or situation and how these thoughts are stirring up the feeling."

2. *Communicate your feelings with words rather than actions.*   In order to work with feelings you have to get them out of your head and out of your gut and put them into words. When many men begin to be more aware of their feelings, they tend to act rather than speak—and even to act in ways that are harmful to others. Avoid this pattern by learning to talk about your feelings in an appropriate manner.

3. *Use "I messages" rather than "you messages."* When your children or your wife act in ways that disturb you, it is usually not helpful to give "you" messages like, "You're stupid" or "You're lazy" or "You think you know everything!" Instead, let your message center on what *you're* feeling: "When you do that, I really get angry," or "When you stay out until 3 A.M. without telling us where you are, I get really worried." This gets the message across without putting the other person on the defensive and destroying their sense of self-worth.

4. *Stick with what's bothering you in the here and now.*   Don't play the role of "historian" and dredge up the irritations or problems of the past. Avoid statements like, "You always . . . " or "You never. . . . " Talk about what is happening now and how you feel about it, why it bothers you and what you would like to see done. This kind of focus encourages problem solving and avoids rehashing old conflicts.

5. *Talk, don't yell.*   Explain what you think and feel without apologizing for it and without defending yourself. But don't use your words to judge or punish others.

6. *Make sure your body language is giving the same message as your voice.* You're standing there with jaws clamped shut, arms crossed tightly across your chest, and your mouth in a thin, tight line. Somebody asks, "What's wrong?" "Nothing!" you mutter. Nobody's going to believe you! You're sending one message with your body and another with your words. Try to bring these two into harmony—and that probably means putting more truth into your words.

The above suggestions apply especially to expressing emotions like anger, anxiety, hurt, or disappointment. It's important to be able to acknowledge your "ownership" of the feeling and to put that feeling into words. If you don't, it will express itself in ways that are more harmful to you and to those around you.

But it is also important to learn to express feelings like love, pride, respect, gratitude, and admiration. You've probably heard of the man who loved his wife so much that he almost told her about it once. Don't wait. Your family and your associates need to hear a good word from you. Take a chance and say, "I appreciate that," "That means a lot to me," or even, "I love you."

Assessing your feelings

Complete the following sentences with your own thoughts. Then rank them from 1 to 12, with 1 being the easiest to share with someone else and 12 being the most difficult. Pay particular attention to any you have difficulty completing. Consider discussing your responses with your spouse or a close friend as a beginning step in learning to talk about your feelings.

____ I am most proud of . . .

____ I get angry when . . .

____ I am happiest when . . .

____ I feel nervous when . . .

____ I get excited when . . .

____ I feel safe when . . .

____ I am hurt when . . .

____ I feel ashamed when . . .

____ I feel loving when . . .

____ I am afraid when . . .

____ I feel guilty when . . .

____ I feel discouraged when . . .

5

Friend and Brother

A man of many companions may come to ruin, but there is a friend who sticks closer than a brother.

Proverbs 18:24

"You know, when I look back on my life as a kid, one of the things I remember most are the friends I had in the old neighborhood, the guys I walked to school with every day and played ball with in the streets every afternoon. We spent whole summers together, planning and carrying out adventures, riding bikes, building tree houses and forts. We were inseparable. They called us the Three Musketeers. We went all through high school together. I wonder whatever happened to those guys?"

Many American men have memories like this. In boyhood most men enjoyed a number of very close friendships. As adults, however, many find themselves without friendships that are satisfying and sustaining.

By contrast, American women are quicker to form friendships, and their friendships run deeper. In the book *Intimate Strangers* psychologist Lillian Rubin reported her study of men and women, ages 25-65, married and single, representing all social classes. Of the single men she interviewed, more than two-thirds could not name a best friend, while two-thirds of the single women could. According to Rubin, "Even when men claimed a best friend, the two shared little about the interior of their lives and feelings. . . . It wasn't unusual to hear a man say he didn't know his friend's marriage was in serious trouble until he appeared one night asking if he could sleep on the couch."

"Men do bond with each other, but it's the kind of nonverbal bonding, a kind of nonverbal attachment. That doesn't feel like intimacy to women, and I don't think it is. There's no reciprocal sharing. They don't share that kind of inner self that two women might share if they were having lunch together."

According to the research, it is especially hard for men to form new friendships after the age of 35. When they attempt to do so, they tend to adopt what psychologists call a "regressive strategy"—recalling the days of their boyhood, they form friendships based on sports or centered around games. A university professor says: "Even when two males build a lasting friendship, its foundation is usually a shared interest in some type of competition, be it occupational or recreational. And that almost always ensures that the relationship will never deepen into intimacy but rather stay at a superficial and guarded level."

It's no wonder that one recent study is entitled *The Friendless American Male*.

Barriers to friendship

Why do men have such difficulty making and keeping friends? What happens in the transition from child to adult that isolates men from one another—and often from women as well? What are the barriers to friendship for men?

1. Our economic system

Our economic system encourages mobility. A man chooses to move for job advancement and higher wages, or he is moved by his corporation, or is forced to move because of changes in the job market. In such a move all he can take with him is his immediate nuclear family. As a result, it becomes difficult to maintain relationships with friends and extended family. If we decide that friendships are important, we may have to stay put, even making financial sacrifices to do that.

While we may have "friends" at work, the work relationship often does not permit true or deep friendships. We may be in competition with the person for job advancement. We may be afraid to reveal certain weaknesses because these might get back to our boss. As a result, coffee-break conversation is often limited to "safe" chatter about professional sports, the latest TV shows, or gas mileage on cars. The unwritten rule seems to be, "No one is allowed to say anything significant."

2. How we grow up

In his book *The Hazards of Being Male* Herb Goldberg maintains that a great part of the problem men have in developing intimate friendships is due to early negative conditioning. The male emphasis on competition, power, and individual performance undermines the development of close relationships that depend on cooperation, sharing, and equality.

This early negative conditioning is in part the result of

expectations that are communicated to boys and men. These expectations militate against the formation of deep friendships. This can be seen even more clearly when we compare society's expectations for men with its expectations for women.

Men in our culture are supposed to be aggressive in the face of attack, independent in problem situations, and sexually aggressive. They suppress strong emotions and are self-reliant, self-confident, assertive, ambitious, and competitive. Among the adjectives used to describe the male "ideal self" are "shrewd," "assertive," "dominating," "competitive," "critical," and "ambitious."

Such an array of characteristics contributes to the development of success and achievement-oriented "controllers," but does not build effective relationships.

In contrast, adjectives that describe the female "ideal self" include *loving, affectionate, sympathetic, generous, sensitive, helpful,* and *considerate.* These qualities describe the kind of person who can enter into and maintain successful relationships. They help to explain why women often are able to form deeper and more lasting friendships than are men.

3. Seeing all relationships in terms of sex

We in the 20th century have learned to see sex lurking in nearly every relationship—between persons of the same sex or the opposite sex. So when we hear of two men rooming together, we wonder whether they are also having sex together. Or when we see a close friendship between a man and a woman, we wonder whether this includes sleeping together.

One result is that many men fear a close relationship with another man, either because they're afraid of appearing homosexual, or they're afraid of getting caught up in a homosexual relationship. Even the third-grader on the playground who hugs a friend is labeled "gay" by his classmates. In our culture many men have to be half-drunk before they can put their arms around one another. Or it is only in the safely "masculine" world of sports where players can hug one another after a winning goal, or where the ritual slap on the fanny is acceptable. This is not true in other cultures, where European men traditionally embrace one another on meeting, or where Asian men who are in no way sexual partners can walk around holding hands. Again, in our society women are much more free to hug one another, room together, dance together.

The fear of sexuality can also inhibit genuine friendships between men and women. We will look at this issue at the end of this chapter.

Reaching out in friendship

If you suspect that your life could be enriched by developing more and deeper friendships, what can you do?

1. Realize how important friendships are for you.

Despite the myth of male independence, we need friends—for our own emotional health and for the sake of our other relationships. A married man may think of his wife as his friend, perhaps his best friend. This is certainly a good thing. Friendship should be an important part of the marriage relationship. But without other close friends (male and female), a man will depend almost totally on his wife for emotional support. This places a large burden on her and may put a strain on the marriage. Because of this, a wife may encourage her husband to make time for friends, and vice versa.

2. *Commit time to your friendships.*

If you would ask most men why they don't spend more time with friends, they would probably answer, "I'm too busy. I spend all my time on the job or with my family." We always find time for what we consider to be really important. If we are convinced that we need friendship, the next step is to set aside time for it.

Ideally this time should go beyond the adult form of children's parallel play—two men engaged side-by-side in golf or racquetball or fixing cars or fishing. It should include some time for the kind of personal sharing that creates the friendships we can call on for emotional support, understanding, or help in a crisis.

In *The Friendless American Male* David W. Smith writes: "Quality relationships take time to develop and attention to maintain. You usually can't develop them the moment you are in dire need of a friend. You need to be forming friendships with many people all through life."

3. *Start in small but definite ways.*

Quality relationships take time. You probably don't have time for many of them. But begin with one friend. Think of a person you would like to spend more time with, someone you think you could open up to. Get together for breakfast or lunch—maybe even once a week. Help one another with yard work or other tasks. Play tennis or handball. A friendship may be based on mutual activity, but also allow time for talk—and not just about last week's football game or the mileage on your Subaru. Find small ways to talk about your wishes, dreams, problems, and feelings.

You may want to begin by resurrecting or rebuilding some old friendships. If your friend lives in another part of the country, surprise him with a long-distance call (a brief one doesn't cost that much, and even a long call may be worth it). Write a letter, or at least a short note. If you travel on business near his area, plan time to stop in. From this foundation of an established friendship, you can go on to make new friends.

4. *Run the risk of being hurt.*

The journey toward friendship is not without its perils. We may reach out toward another person, in the hopes of developing a friendship, and learn that he is "too busy" or just not interested. Our motives may be misunderstood. It's possible that that person may be embarrassed or not know how to react if we begin talking about feelings or problems.

But the risk is worth it. Even if we get rebuffed, we will have made a breakthrough in our own behavior, and that will make it easier next time. But it is even more likely that the other man will respond, perhaps tentatively at first, and both of you will begin to develop a health-giving relationship. One counselor who works with singles tells them that unless they make at least four attempts at initiating a personal contact with a particular person, they haven't tried hard enough.

5. *Express your friendships in words and actions.*

As we've seen, most of us have been brought up to think that the expression of tenderness or affection is unmasculine. It may feel very awkward for us to express love for another man in words or in gestures. Yet for our own sake, and also for his, it's worth trying to change, even though it may be embarrassing or even painful at first.

This doesn't mean that you have to change your whole personality overnight. That probably isn't possible. Although some men have learned to hug others, you may not turn into the "mad hugger" after reading this book. But you can learn to express love in ways that feel appropriate for you and your friend. It may be with actions, like a handshake, a pat on the back, or a hand on a man's shoulder. Or it may be with words: "You know, I like you. I'm glad you're my friend."

6. *Give your friends room to be themselves.*

Some men have a strong need to dominate and control others. This need may carry over into friendships, and when it does, it usually cuts short the relationship. Dominating men often move from person to person. They have little difficulty finding potential friends, but have a hard time keeping them. Other men, particularly, are sensitive to the control issue and are therefore likely to avoid such an unequal situation.

If you recognize in yourself that need to criticize, "fix," or control a potential friend, you may have to remind yourself to give your friend room to be his own man. This means focusing on the friend's needs and feelings rather than on your own ideas or standards. In the best of friendships the concern is mutual, and this sensitivity to the needs of another, the encouragement of other friendships, and the ability to accommodate and grow with the relationship over time is the cement that seals friendships for a lifetime.

The female friend

So far in this chapter we have been talking mainly about friendship between men. Friendships with women are important too, and for married men as well. It is possible for a married man to have female friends other than his wife, though there are dangers involved. While it may be natural for us to find certain women attractive as friends, and as females, for the sake of our marriages and families we have to use some common sense.

In *The Friendship Factor* Alan Loy McGinnis suggests six guidelines for keeping sexual feelings under control while still enjoying friendships with members of the opposite sex:

1. Don't trust yourself too far. Be aware of the ebb and flow of your sexual desire. Most of us vary greatly in the amount of sexual feeling we have, and at times its power can rush in on us if we are not prepared. If your sexuality is at flood tide, then exercise extra caution.

2. Select companions who have strong marriages themselves. If your friend is hungry for love, it may be very difficult to keep the relationship within bounds.

3. Be sensible about when and where you meet alone. Some settings are more sexual than others. Lunch, for instance, is not as likely to lead to trouble as dinner at a restaurant filled with lovers eating by candlelight.

4. Talk to your mate about your friendships. When meetings become clandestine, it is a danger signal that things are getting out of hand. Either bring yourself to tell your spouse about the progression of the friendship or get out.

5. Draw a line for physical contact. Find the amount of physical affection that is comfortable and safe

for you, since no one can stay in control once sexual touching and kissing cross a certain boundary.

6. Bail out if necessary. Once in a while, no matter how much we try, a friendship with the opposite sex gets out of hand and we know where it is going to lead. If your marriage is precious to you, there is no question of what must be done, however great the pain—you back away.

The friendship journey

Out of the brokenness that has characterized their relationships in the past, many men today are learning to build a sense of brotherhood with one another. "Journeymen" are exploring new ways of relating and of solving problems.

One way this is being accomplished is by men talking more openly among themselves about issues that have created conflict. Men's growth and support groups are gaining greater acceptance as men have begun to see the need for creating caring relationships with one another. Some of these groups have been organized around a shared interest or concern (Bible studies, book clubs). Others have been more open-ended and have focused on the discussion of personal issues and concerns.

Conferences and workshops addressing the issues facing today's men have become more frequent and better attended. Books and articles have created greater awareness of men's problems and have made suggestions for change.

A great many men have started on the journey inward. New paths are being explored. Other men will join along the way. It's an exciting and important trip!

Roster of fellow travelers

Write in the names of persons who:

- I can reveal myself to:
- I can let go of the need to control things with:

- I can have fun playing with:
- I feel in partnership with:
- I can ask help from:
- I don't need to compete with:

My friendship response

For each of the statements below, put a check mark in the column that most accurately indicates where you now are in the different aspects of friendship.

	No Problem	Working at it	Need help
Relationship priority			
1. When I experience personal problems, I can call on at least one other person.			
2. I keep in touch with friends from the past by calling or writing.			
3. I am interested in other people's lives and look for opportunities to make new friends.			
4. I have at least three people (other than spouse or family) I can share recreational play with.			

	No Problem	Working at it	Need help

Practicing openness
1. I work at sharing my emotions with others.
2. I have at least one friend with whom I can say almost anything.
3. I ask for help from people outside my immediate family.
4. I can accept what others say to me and about me without getting defensive.

Communicating friendship
1. I can show affection to another male friend in public without embarrassment.
2. On my own initiative I have bought or made a gift for a friend in the past year.
3. I make regular plans to spend time with friends.
4. I tell my friends that I like them and that they are important to me.

Making room
1. I encourage friends to be who they are, not who I am.
2. I do not attempt to dominate my friends' time, nor do I expect to be their only friend.
3. Things don't always have to go my way.
4. I can tolerate some disagreement, disinterest, and defects in my friendships.

6

Work: Frustration or Fulfillment

To do our duty in our own sphere, to try to create something worth creating, as our life's work, is the way to understand what joy is in this life.   *W. R. Inge*

Harold sat alone in his golf cart, impeccably dressed in matched cashmere sweater and slacks. Across the back of his cart lay one set of clubs, custom-made and personally fitted, the best money could buy.

The first tee at the country club bustled with Saturday activity. A few members called out, "Hi, Harold, how's it going?" but none stopped to talk. Tension seemed to exist between the other men and this imposing but solitary figure.

It was clear that he was playing alone, but no one invited him to play along. The foursomes were set, but Harold sat off to the side, waiting for his own private tee-off time.

Later, one of the senior members of the club was asked about Harold, so isolated in the midst of many people who seemed to know him. He said that Harold was one of the most successful men in the community—and one of the most disliked. A local architect, he had been involved in almost every major construction project in the area in the past 30 years. One of the largest holders of real estate in the city, he wielded great personal influence. He had the reputation for being ambitious, tough, competitive, work-addicted, and unprincipled in his dealings with others. He had labored 60-70 hours a week for years, building his business and amassing a personal fortune. In the process he had lost his wife and children and alienated most of his friends and associates.

Now at age 60 Harold had most of what he wanted: material wealth, power, and influence. But no one wanted him. A lonely, isolated man, he played alone on weekends with no one to share what he had. He had made work his idol, and it turned out to have feet of clay. His addiction to work had become a lifelong rut. Maybe—just, maybe—someday Harold will ask himself, "What went wrong?"

The importance of work

Although Harold's life is an extreme case, it illustrates the importance of work for men in our culture. A man's work, perhaps more than anything else, defines who he is. When men meet, one of the first things they ask is, "What do you do?" For most men, the answer to that question determines how the two men will relate to one another. Job title, responsibility, and income immediately place men somewhere in an invisible hierarchy that dictates position, status, and power.

More than that, on the positive side, work can be a major—maybe even the principal—way in which a man finds meaning in life. Psychiatrist Viktor Frankl pointed out that one of the deepest drives for all people is the search for meaning. This drive may be even stronger than the drive for power, the desire for sex, or physical hunger. Work, Frankl said, is usually the area in which an individual's uniqueness stands in relation to society, thus giving life meaning and value.

Work is an important bond that holds people together, connecting them in unique ways. Many men have their only meaningful relationships—beyond their families—at work. When pursued in healthy ways, work can provide opportunities for cooperative effort, sharing, and comradeship.

When we consider that a man spends approximately one-third of his life as a worker, and when we add to that figure the amount of time spent in education for work, training for work, and talking, thinking, and worrying about work, it is clear that a man's job plays a crucial role in his life.

Problems in the work world

Despite all their efforts, many men do not find satisfaction through their work. What goes wrong?

1. Work addiction

While work plays a crucial role in a man's life, it is not meant to be all of life. Yet because of certain expectations placed on men, work all too often becomes the single focus.

The heavy emphasis on achievement and performance in our society may push a man in this direction. Some men may compensate for feelings of inadequacy in other areas by focusing on success in their work. These compulsive workers become overinvolved in their jobs, often as a way of avoiding emotional closeness to others. Because their hours tend to be long and irregular and they are often traveling on business, they seldom have a chance to spend time with family and friends or engage in leisure activities. Such men often get "antsy" when they have nothing to do. They usually have few hobbies or interests other than their work, and they can't imagine being retired—for they have no idea what they would do if they were not working.

This single-minded drive for success in work is also fostered by the success formulas we pick up from the world of professional sports. Pro football, in particular, has promulgated a philosophy of winning at all costs and success through dominance and intimidation. Vince Lombardi is quoted as having said, "Winning isn't the most important thing. It's the only thing."

A man who is driven in his work (even when that work is important for the welfare of others) risks himself and his purpose in life. More and more men are finding themselves unable to function indefinitely at a pace and in a manner that is literally life-threatening.

Considerable investigation of the so-called Type A personality—characterized by restlessness, impatience, constant striving for achievement, and extreme competitiveness—has revealed a much higher likelihood of coronary disease and other stress-related illnesses in men who fit this category.

There are also indications that work-addicted men experience more frustration because of their attitudes toward work. Psychologist Robert Veninga suggests that workaholics experience frustration in three ways:

1. They want others to share their extreme dedication to work. When this doesn't happen, they be-

come resentful and blame others for "not pulling their weight."

2. They find it difficult to consider the psychological needs of their family members and friends. Work is considered the most important activity. In time family members feel ignored and angry, especially if home has become only a stopping-off place between one business meeting and another.

3. Workaholics can become mentally fatigued because they have given little effort to self-renewal. [The many books and articles on "burnout" reveal how common that experience is.]

2. Facing the trauma of unemployment

When a man finds nearly all his life meaning in his work, what does he do when he is suddenly out of a job? Getting fired, being laid off, or changing careers often brings feelings of anger, frustration, fear, embarrassment, and low self-esteem.

George had worked for more than 20 years for the same engineering firm. When a deep economic recession set in he found himself with no job—and with no immediate prospects of regaining his old job. George's wife encouraged him to go to the local university for career evaluation and job counseling, but he couldn't face up to the prospect. He was too depressed to do anything.

In *The Doctor and the Soul* Viktor Frankl described *unemployment neurosis* and its chief symptom—apathy. Having no work, an unemployed man feels useless, empty, and without meaning in life. The longer he stays in that condition, the less likely he is to be able to extricate himself from it.

By contrast, Frankl noted that some unemployed people, facing the same financial pressures, remained serene and even cheerful. They did this by filling their newfound time with volunteer work, reading, leisure activities, and education. Said Frankl, "They have grasped the fact that the meaning of human life is not completely contained within paid work, that unemployment need not compel one to live meaninglessly. They have stopped making an equation between living and having a job."

3. Coping with retirement

If temporary unemployment causes severe problems for a work-dominated person, retirement or permanent unemployment may generate the kind of crisis that causes some men, consciously or unconsciously, to give up on life. The man who has devoted his whole life to work, developing no other hobbies or interests along the way, often finds himself dreading retirement, wondering what in the world he is going to do with all that time. On the other hand, the journeyman who has traveled some of life's "blue highways" has many things he still wants to do, and he can look forward to an exciting new chapter of life.

4. The trap of meaningless work

Frankl pointed out that a man can be capable of working and still not lead a meaningful life. Lack of education or training may keep a man in a job that does not make full use of his gifts. Sometimes an early job choice no longer provides the incentive it once did. A study by the research firm of Yankelovich, Skelly, and White says that only one in four Americans finds fulfillment at work.

Charles, born into a blue-collar family with little money, decided at age 18 that he would opt for financial security. His parents encouraged him in his decision to become a dentist. For 20 years he found some satisfaction and meaning in his work, but then felt like the bottom dropped out. Each day became a chore to be dreaded. He desperately wanted to make a job change, but at his age, with one child in college and two more close behind, he felt a change was impossible.

Elton Trueblood writes, "The man who stays in the secure path, never making the break in the direction of his real interest or sense of calling, will become an increasingly unhappy and frustrated man. The way of wisdom is to make the break and to make it at once in spite of difficulties and temporary or permanent sacrifice. The sense of using one's life rightly is so important that real sacrifice, even on the part of the rest of the family, is wholly justified."

If a man genuinely decides that a job change is impossible because of economic or other reasons, then it is imperative that he find meaning in another sector of his life. (The next chapter, "Learning to Play Again," will provide some guidance in this area.)

5. *The changing job picture*

In our rapidly changing world there will continue to be frequent shifts in the work picture. Some of these will cause additional pressures for the traditional male; others will provide opportunities for new and more healthful ways of living and working.

As the recent economic depression showed, the men hardest hit are often those in traditionally masculine jobs such as construction and heavy manufacturing. Economists point out that the most rapidly growing area of the economy is the service sector.

Tom, who had been making $14 an hour as a New Jersey steel worker, is now earning $4.75 as custodian in a state office building. "I had a challenging job," he said, "but now I just have something to do. Finding a job is hard, but finding a good job is really hard."

For many men, the question remains, Will I be able to shift from *making* and *doing* to serving others?

While women are moving into jobs once dominated by men, males are taking work in traditionally female fields. According to a recent report the number of male nurses increased by 140 percent between 1972 and 1980. The proportion of men working as telephone operators nearly tripled in the same period. The percentage of male airline cabin attendants has quadrupled.

While such jobs may require a man to rethink his masculine identity, many men are finding that the rewards are worth it. A job as a secretary may be a stepping stone to an administrative slot. Teaching young children may give a sense of satisfaction and self-worth.

Working with today's women

One of the biggest changes in the workplace has been the presence of women—especially more assertive women. For many men this new situation presents challenges that require shifts in attitude and style.

Complaints of sexual harassment, unequal treatment, and discriminatory practices seem to be on the increase as more women enter the still male-dominated and controlled work setting. Some studies suggest that most men are too competitive to find happiness in a female partner's success, and that many men are threatened by women in the workplace.

Such men continue to have difficulty granting equal status to women on the job, even to those who have commensurate education, training, and ability. This attitude fuels women's resentment toward men who, they feel, use their power and position to control and discriminate against them. Today a large number of women feel that, at best, men are antagonistic toward them in their work settings, and at worst deliberately exploit them.

Some of the specific concerns often voiced by women deal with practices such as:

- paying an equally trained and experienced woman at a lower rate than a man for the same job responsibilities;
- implying without adequate justification that a woman is not as good a decision maker as a man or that she would be unable to supervise men effectively;
- being called a "girl" on the job, regardless of how menial the position. One woman explained it this way: "Women don't want to be called *girl* for the same reasons most black men don't want to be called *boy*."
- always designating a woman in a predominantly male working group as the note-taker or secretary;
- routinely assigning the responsibility for making and serving coffee, bringing food, and cleaning up afterward to the women in a group.

While some women are still facing discrimination on the job, today the shoe is sometimes on the other foot.

Robert, a 49-year-old librarian, reported, "I'm in what is basically a woman's profession. In the past this was an advantage for me, because a man was more likely to be advanced into an administrative position. Today, all things being equal between a male and a female candidate, the woman is more likely to get the promotion."

Stan, who has worked 20 years for a large corporation, now sees himself being passed over for promotion in favor of women who are less experienced and less qualified. "It's hard," he admits.

Kevin, a college professor, says that in his field right now, "for the white male the job opportunities are zero."

Current attempts to bring about more balance between men and women in the work force will inevitably create tensions and pain for some men. Some men may have to adjust their attitudes toward success and "climbing the ladder." It may also mean finding a sense of self-worth in areas of life besides the marketplace.

Men are also finding that some women today have considerable difficulty working with men—any men. They have difficulty receiving criticism from men and every issue is seen as a male-female confrontation. Doug, copy chief in a large advertising agency, faced this problem with a competent, but always antagonistic, female copywriter. "Finally one day," he said, "I took her in my office and said, 'Hey, it seems that we're having a hard time working together. Let's see if we can figure out why.' That opened the way for talking about the male-female issues that lay behind some of our work conflicts. Things have gone better since then."

Suggestions for low-stress working

Since most of us, whether we like it or not, spend a major part of our lives working, we may as well learn to do it in ways that *decrease* frustration and *increase* fulfillment. Here are some suggestions.

1. Don't let your work dominate your entire life.
2. In the course of your work, build cooperative, pleasant relationships with as many of your coworkers or employees as you can.
3. Rank your work tasks in order of importance and

manage your time effectively. Try not to take on more than you can handle.

4. Whenever possible, take the initiative rather than letting your work dictate to you.

5. Build an effective and supportive relationship with your boss. Understand his or her problems and help your boss to understand yours.

6. Study the future. Learn as much as you can about likely coming events that may affect your job and your work.

7. If your job allows for it, find some time every day for detachment and relaxation. Take a walk now and then to keep your body refreshed and alert. Greet people you meet along the way.

8. If you supervise others in your work, make sure you know how to delegate effectively. Keep track of a typical day's work and see how many things you do that are really part of someone else's job.

9. Don't put off dealing with distasteful problems such as resolving conflicts on the job or straightening out a relationship problem with a coworker.

10. Make a constructive "worry list." Write down the problems that concern you about your job and something that can be done about each one of them. Get them out in the open where you can deal with them.

11. If you are unhappy with your job or your employer, do something constructive about changing the situation. If this is not possible, concentrate on the quality of your performance. How can you polish and improve yourself and your skills and abilities for some future opportunity?

7

Learning to Play Again

If I had only . . .
forgotten future greatness
and looked at the green things and the buildings
and reached out to those around me
and smelled the air
and ignored the forms and the self-styled obligations
and heard the rain on the roof
and put my arms around my wife
. . . and it's not too late.

Hugh Prather

The pursuit of personal ambitions and career goals requires great commitments of time and effort. For many men who are committed to this path, leisure time is seen as something to be enjoyed only if the pursuit of their primary goals allows for it.

Such an attitude may already be outdated. In his book *Megatrends* John Naisbitt points out that over the past century the average work week has dropped from 73 to 35 hours. He forecasts that it will be halved again in half the time, projecting a 17-hour work week within the next 50 years. As men cope with a shorter work week, a shared-work arrangement with a wife, and earlier retirement, the ability to make effective use of leisure time will become a valuable skill.

The traditional performance-oriented man needs to learn that the creative use of play and leisure time can be refreshing and revitalizing, and life-lengthening as well. He needs to see that doing things "just for the fun of it," with a lighthearted, easy-going attitude will help him to manage stress and allow him to look to the future with energy and optimism. Those who cannot make this important shift are likely to become one-dimensional persons. They run the risk of alienation from others, increased resentment over life's responsibilities, and problems with retirement.

Webster defines leisure time as "free, unoccupied time during which a person may indulge in rest and recreation." The problem for some men has been the way they have defined "rest and recreation" and the degree to which they have "indulged" in these activities. Can leisure time be wasted? Can it be destructive to a man? The answer to both questions is yes.

Leisure time as wasted time

Excessive drinking is one of the most common ways in which men abuse leisure time. It is difficult to estimate the number of men who qualify as "weekend alcoholics," but the figure would be high. Men who seldom if ever miss a day of work and who may not even touch a drink during the week may drink to excess on weekends, abusing their physical and emotional health and deeply injuring their family relationships. A physician commented, "Maybe it is important to see why men drink in bars. It's a relaxed 'man's' atmosphere. It provides acceptance and male friendships. And the bartender is a sympathetic, nonthreatening, nonconfronting listener." The challenge is for men to learn to meet these real needs in healthier ways. Of course many men do their weekend drinking at home. This may suggest problems beyond the need for friendship, socialization, and a listening ear. It may be a way of escaping from family relationships or avoiding family tensions.

Another escapist misuse of leisure time is excessive TV watching. For too many men, the primary leisure activity is flopping down in front of the TV, with or without a can of beer. In particular, *watching* sports has become the national pastime for a vast number of American men who spend their weekends staring at the television set. And now a cable hookup permits round-the-clock sports.

What's so bad about watching sports on TV? In itself, nothing, but when it occupies nearly all of a man's leisure time, it leads to several problems.

For one thing, such preoccupation may seriously damage a man's relationship with his wife and children. As one wife put it, "I try to talk with him and he tells me, 'Not now. The game is on.' I wait for the intermission and try again, and he still won't respond. He even has favorite commercials he watches."

Excessive TV-watching fills time that could be used for more active, meaningful—and therefore ultimately more rewarding—activities.

Frank, age 36, reports what happened to him one day. "I watched one basketball game, and then another game came on. I thought, 'I'm going to sit here for another hour and a half wasting my time watching this game? I could read about it in the paper tomorrow and be just as happy.'

So I shut off the TV, went to the Y and swam and ran for two hours. I got back just in time to see the last shot. I felt good because I'd done something with the two hours instead of sitting there for the whole time just to see that last ten-second shot."

If you've gotten trapped into TV addiction, you might try a few tricks for escaping the tube. One solution is to choose to limit your TV watching to a certain number of hours a week. Another is to commit yourself to spending one hour at some more active pastime for each hour of TV watching, activities like physical exercise, reading, taking a walk, volunteer work, or talking to family and friends.

Leisure time as performance

Some men bring the same driven quality to their play that they experience at work. They play 36 holes of golf, rain or shine. They force themselves to run a certain number of miles a day at a required, predetermined pace. When they play tennis or handball it's always "for blood," with an attempt to drive the ball down the teeth of their opponent. We call these men "Type A at play."

These men find some release by engaging in a different form of activity and they do receive some benefits from the exercise. But they experience little of the sense of freedom or release provided by a more healthy form of play. For them, leisure becomes another demand, another schedule, another challenge, another competitor to overcome. Instead of taking a break from pressure, they work hard at their play and succeed only in increasing their tension and stress.

This type of man often becomes a compulsive fitness buff. Some research suggests that a man in his 30s is most likely to become compulsive about exercise. Because our culture values physical prowess in men, men tend to define themselves by their physical capabilities. Somewhere in his 30s a man begins to be concerned about his waning physical powers. At this point he may choose (often unconsciously) to make a last-ditch effort to renew these powers, or at least to keep them from slipping further.

These "Type A at play" individuals are in a sense negatively addicted to a pattern of exercise and a use of leisure time that may be potentially destructive. They start sailing for the pure joy of it and before long have to race and win. They begin to run a mile or two a day because they want to stay trim and enjoy the outdoors, and the next thing they know they are training for a marathon. It's easy for men to get caught up in the performance, competition, and mastery of games, all of which tends to move the playful use of leisure back into the area of work, duty, and obligation.

Stu Mittelman, America's record holder for the 100-mile run, suggests that by following a few principles we can sidestep the obsession with competition and learn to really enjoy sports:

1. Forget the idea that "winners never quit and quitters never win." It can lead you into serious injury. A better proposition is, "Winners know when to quit; losers never try."

2. Abandon the idea of "no pain, no gain." A certain amount of pain may be necessary in your development as an athlete, but ignoring all pain signals is foolish. Instead, says Mittelman, "Learn from your pain—and allow yourself to feel good."

3. Realize that you are not a professional athlete who must win all the time because it's his job. For most of us, winning is *not* everything. It may be one of

only several goals, including long-term health and well-being.

Learning to play again

How can you learn to play again in ways that are healthful, enjoyable, and beneficial? It's important that you find your own way in this, rather than trying to live up to expectations set by someone else, but here are a few tips:

Recognize with gratitude that you have a need and a right to play. Remind yourself of this if you start feeling guilty because you're not working.

Find ways of playing that you genuinely enjoy. Make a game of trying to find new ways to enjoy life. Challenge yourself to try one new sport every year. Try to learn a new game every three months. Play a musical instrument or sing in a choir or barbershop quartet. Improve your swimming. Take a class at your community college. Join a book discussion group. Begin a new hobby. The possibilities are endless. Search for the ones that give you the most fun.

In choosing from among the many possibilities, give preference to the active rather than the passive (within your physical limitations, of course). Instead of watching someone else play tennis on TV, get out there and play a few sets. Instead of sitting in the audience at a concert, take out your old instrument and join a community orchestra. Instead of reading another mystery, sign up for a creative writing course and write your own. You might surprise yourself!

While we may think we're too tired and may just feel like collapsing in front of the TV, we will find that we have more energy if we do something active. Vigorous physical activity, a creative hobby, or participation with other people will actually generate energy and give us greater zest for life.

Ideas for low-stress living

In connection with the topic of leisure, we'd like to suggest the following ideas to help you manage stress and live in a more leisurely way.

1. Make time your ally, not your master. Invest in a daily planning guide. Create a realistic schedule for work, and reserve prime time for family, leisure, and service projects.
2. Seek out a few gentle people who affirm you as a person.
3. Form at least one or two high-quality relationships with people you trust and with whom you can be yourself.
4. Think and act positively. The worst thing that can happen rarely does.
5. Seek out interesting and rewarding experiences. Try doing things that are new to you. Sample foods you have never eaten. Go places you have never been.
6. Listen to the ideas and opinions of others and learn from them. Read interesting books and articles to freshen your ideas and broaden your points of view. Avoid "psychosclerosis" (also known as "hardening of categories").
7. Have one or more pastimes that give you a chance to do something relaxing without having to have something to show for it.
8. Don't drift along in troublesome and stressful situations. Rehabilitate a bad marriage. Resolve problems with friends or family. Take action to settle those matters that are troubling you. Don't let problem situations go on unattended for so

long that they make you chronically worried and tense.

9. Protect your personal freedoms: the freedom to choose your friends, the freedom to care for whom you choose, the freedom to structure your time as you see fit, the freedom to set your own life goals.

10. Maintain "stability zones"—positive personal habits and patterns that serve as insulators and reduce the jostling and buffeting of life.

11. Give some time and effort in service to another person or group, your church perhaps. Exclusive focus on yourself and your own needs and feelings is a dead end.

12. Find some time every day, even if only 10 minutes, for complete privacy, when you can be alone with your thoughts, free from the pressures of work and responsibility.

Build your leisure time into your schedule. If you don't, the time will quickly fill up with work or with time-wasters. Mark your leisure time activities on your weekly calendar. (They are that important!) At the same time, be alert to opportunities that can be seized at the moment: walking in the woods on a crisp autumn day, taking a nap on a rainy afternoon, or making a snowman with the kids.

8

The Women in Your Life

To be a man is to possess the strength to love another, not the need to dominate over others.

David Augsburger

The major thrust of this book is that men are caught in the middle of change. Nowhere is this more true than in their relationships with women. Simply put, women are changing, and as a result men can no longer stay the same. The story of Carl and Lois will help shed some light on what we mean.

A man and his marriage

The final divorce papers were delivered to Carl's new address. After 14 years of marriage, he still wasn't sure what had happened.

In his mind, Lois had changed over the past few years. She was so different from the person he had first married. It seemed that she was no longer content with their life together. The worst of it had come when she started to work. He hadn't wanted that. His job had provided the family with all the material things it needed and more. But there was no reasoning with her. She had said something about needing to grow. He asked her why she couldn't do that at home, and she had looked at him as if he had come from another planet.

Everything seemed to change after that. She didn't cook as much, and there were times when he even had to press his own shirt before going to work in the morning. He began to feel that their problem was "the women's lib thing." They fought about the kids more and about who would take care of responsibilities around the house. They began to quarrel about sex, too. Carl suspected another man, and he began to check up on Lois. He even followed her once to try to confirm his suspicions. Eventually lawyers got involved, and that was the beginning of the end.

Lois told a somewhat different story. She complained bitterly about the "one-sidedness" of their relationship from the very beginning. Carl's needs, job, and career always had to be considered first. She related her frustration at having to raise three children with little or no emotional involvement from Carl. Yes, the bills had always been paid and the family had all the material things it needed. But they had not had a husband or father who had been there in the way he was needed most.

What had hurt her more than anything else had been Carl's insensitivity to her needs as a person. She resented his condescending attitude toward her, the way he always devalued her ideas and opinions. How surprised she had been at her job to find that men and women alike paid attention to her and found merit in what she had to say. Carl seemed threatened by her need to grow. Yet the more he tried to control and restrict her, the more she wanted to be free. She summed it up this way: "I just wanted something for myself. I wanted to be more than just Carl's wife. I wanted to be my own person. He never really understood that."

There is no good guy or bad guy in this story, just two people who became hurt and alienated from one another, and a family that will never again be whole.

Lois was driven by a need to change a relationship that wasn't working for her because it no longer affirmed her as an individual. Certainly the "women's lib thing," as Carl called it, had something to do with Lois' greater awareness of herself and her potential as an individual person. But this heightened awareness and need for clearer self-definition might not have preceded a disaster if Carl could have responded in a more balanced way. If he had been able to help rather than hinder Lois' growth, that might have led to healthy changes—not only for Lois, but for the marriage as well. What Carl failed to see was that Lois had stopped trying to live up (or down) to his distortion of who or what she should be like. For her, the issue had not been separateness and independence, but the need for a greater sense of personhood and equality in the relationship.

Changing the patterns

Change is never easy. Some men have not had the kind of early experiences or role models that would make it easy for them to follow a new path in their life. Carl may have had trouble understanding and relating to Lois' need for personal growth because he grew up in a family where a man's and a woman's role were traditional, stereotyped ones. He was not prepared for the changes that he would encounter in his own marriage. He may not have had a father who modeled tolerance, understanding, and sensitivity to a woman's needs. If, in fact, this was the case, he would not have been very different from many of his contemporaries. Men today are on the growing edge in a rapidly changing world. This is a precarious position, but not an impossible one. Someone has said, "When you're through changing, you're through!" We don't think men are through yet.

Earlier we touched on some characteristic ways men approach the world. We spoke of a need for them to learn how to balance power with mutuality, dominance with equality, and competition with cooperation in their relationships with others. When we apply these dichotomies to how a man relates to women in his life, we begin to see some of the changes and adjustments that need to be made.

Sydney J. Harris said, "Dominance makes a ruling group stupid." More men are beginning to learn that a position of unconditional authority and power has no place in an intimate relationship. In fact, such a position prevents intimacy from developing between two people. It is not helpful for a man to block close personal feelings by refusing to see the needs of another as equal to his own. Getting along with someone else, whether it be on the job, in a family, or in a marriage, requires a willingness to give and take. One journeyman related the success he was now experiencing in his marriage relationship to this give-and-take process. "Almost everything in a marriage relationship has to be negotiable. And those things that aren't, you need to lay those out as such. Negotiation makes our marriage work well. Whatever you need, you have to make it known to the other person and they have to see if they can help with it. If not, they have to say so."

There is also some research evidence to suggest that if men and women can make the kind of changes that will allow them to adapt to the demands of today's world, there is help on the way. Cross-cultural studies by Professor David Gutmann indicate that as men and women get older, there is a period, usually in middle life, when they become more like one another and adopt traits and characteristics usually associated with the opposite sex. In her book *Pathfinders* Gail Sheehy summarizes this shift: "Each becomes something of what the other used to be—the woman more independent and strong-minded, the man more emotionally responsive and interested in human attachments."

While some men—and women—may be threatened by this shift, an ability to embrace both dimensions of ourselves, the "masculine" and the "feminine" sides, contributes greatly to our personal growth and self-fulfillment. When all aspects of our personality are valued and accepted rather than rejected and denied, we will possess a greater capacity to see the complementaries in one another rather than the conflicts.

From such a position, a man is still a man, but he is more than that. He is a sensitive and caring human being who can permit himself to feel and relate on an intimate level. He is able to recognize that he can learn much from a woman about how to live with and through his feelings as well as his intellect. And he knows that he has things to teach a woman, also. This kind of openness and acceptance might have helped avoid the tragedy and pain in the lives of Carl and Lois.

Who's boss?

In response to the women's movement, some men and groups of men have reasserted the traditional supremacy of males. Books have been written with titles like *The Inevitability of Patriarchy.* Some men look at the European or Japanese pattern of male-female relationships and there find some hope of stemming the tide. This appears to be a losing battle, because it flies in the face of major social changes.

Among those reacting against the new independence and assertiveness of women are certain religious groups. In publications and through teaching seminars they emphasize that the man is ordained by God to be the head of the family. God's intention is that a wife be obedient and submissive. The man has the right and the duty to take charge and make the decisions. He should never wash dishes or change a diaper, because these are tasks God intended for women. In general, a man today should act as most males did in America a generation or two ago.

These conservative arguments for the supremacy of men are based on Bible passages like Eph. 5:22: "Wives, be subject to your husbands, as to the Lord. For the husband is the head of the wife as Christ is the head of the church, his body, and is himself its Savior." The debate over passages like this goes on. How much of it is meant for a specific time in history, and how much is meant to apply to all time? How do we apply first-century statements to our changed situation? For men who regard the Bible as the authoritative Word of God, these questions cannot just be brushed off.

We asked one pastor how he handles this issue. He said, "The Bible does say that the husband is to be the head of the wife. But headship is always seen in terms of service rather than authority. The question is not who is the boss, but who is the servant. The husband is to serve his wife and children as Christ served the church and gave himself for it. A man has no right to use this passage to maintain a dictatorship in the family. And he shouldn't hide behind the Bible to avoid doing his fair share of the work around the house. Jesus said that if we want to be great in the kingdom of God, we should be the ones who serve the most."

For many families the question of who's boss never comes up. Decisions are made mutually. Bob said, "Whoever is most affected by the decision or whoever cares the most should decide. If that's the woman, she should be able to make the decision."

A man and his mother

Some women say they can predict how a man will react in a relationship with them. "The way he responds to and treats his mother is likely to be the way he will respond to and treat me."

Certainly this is not inevitable. But there is some truth in the comparison. At least a man's relationship with his mother does establish some expectations about how women will react to and treat him and how he will be expected to respond. It is usually through this first relationship with a woman that a man is indirectly taught the softer, more feminine side of himself, those qualities that balance off the harder, rougher edges of his maleness.

Of course the impact of a mother on a son is not always positive. For example, a man who has been overindulged by his mother often expects other women, particularly his wife, to treat him in the same way. Some maintain that it is exactly this kind of expectation that has led to disruption of the more traditional marriage—especially when the women in these relationships become aware of a need for more equality and self-development.

One woman was surprised after her marriage when her husband consistently left his dirty underwear on the bedroom floor. When she complained, he said, "But my mother always picked up my underwear." This problem of expectations, carried over from our family of origin, is particularly acute when one's spouse comes to the marriage with a different—or worse, a contradictory—expectation. For example, "Not only did my father not leave his dirty clothes laying around the floor, he did his own laundry!"

Many women justifiably complain, "He wants me to treat him the way his mother did: cook and clean for him, indulge him and accept his little misbehaviors, like staying out late with other 'boys' or spending all day Sunday watching football on TV. I'm tired of it. I don't need another child. I want a husband and a friend, someone who will give something to me too."

A man and his sexuality

Sexuality can create problems for some men because of the conflicts it stirs up within them. One of these conflicts involves the ambivalent way in which many men have come to view women. Men have been raised with the attitude that women (like mothers) are to be revered and protected. They have come to believe that women are more fragile, and less sexual than men. "Good girls," those who are considered marriage prospects, are still expected to be virginal and inhibited where sex is concerned. At the same time, books, movies, and television often present women as something quite different. Beauty contests and the advertising media emphasize women as sex objects. As a result, men are often confused as to how to respond to women, and often treat them in highly inconsistent ways.

A second problem in the area of sexuality for a man is the emphasis placed on his own performance and the cultural stereotype of a desirable male as one who is aggressive and virile. The unspoken expectation is that a man will always be "ready, willing, and able" to perform sexually (no headaches allowed here). And if he is not, there must be something wrong with him. In the confines of such a restricted view, there isn't much room for individual variability, and little if any opportunity for a man to develop a realistic attitude toward his capabilities and limitations.

Some of the changes that women have been experiencing over the past several years have contributed to additional problems for men in the sexual area. Partly as a result of more effective means of birth control and contemporary attitudes of our society, women are experiencing a newfound sense of freedom and a healthier view of their own sexuality. These changes have left some men, especially those already laboring under a heavy performance expectation, even more threatened and uncomfortable about their abilities. "How do I respond to my wife's more assertive expression of her sexuality? Can I satisfy her needs? What will she think of me if I can't?" These are questions many men face with uncertainty.

We have discussed the need for a man to embark on an inner journey that allows him to explore some alternative ways of thinking and being. One of these alternative paths involves giving up a single-minded focus on performance and control and exploring the possibility of "letting go and letting be." Relinquishing an excessive need for control would help a man experience a greater sense of playfulness in his relationships. Spontaneous enjoyment rather than rigid, goal-oriented performance would allow a man to develop a deeper and more satisfying sexual life. Released from a single-minded focus on *doing*, men would be able to pay more attention to their own feelings and experiences as well as their partner's.

But how can a man make that kind of shift? How does he let go and let be rather than continue blindly down the performance and control path—a path strewn with unrealistic expectations and pressures to be what someone else wants rather than who he is? A first step is to risk opening up and talking about some fears and uncertainties in sexual matters:

In the beginning, we didn't talk about our sexual relationship at all. It was something that was confined to the bedroom and that was it. When we did start talking more, it was hard for me at first, especially telling her things that seemed like my problem, like that I wasn't always turned on and sometimes could care less about having sex. I wondered what she would think. But when she said she'd be more worried about me if I were interested in sex every minute, I laughed. I realized that was exactly how I thought I should be, and I just assumed she expected it too.

Another man said, "I was helped by the idea that either sexual partner should be free to initiate sex, or refuse it, or fail at it."

An even further step might be to see that the idea of "failure" does not apply to sex. We can learn to accept what does happen and enjoy it—even though it doesn't result in the perfectly timed mutual orgasm.

Impotence—the inability to achieve an erection 25 percent of the time—has been called "the problem men worry about most." While impotence can be caused by physical conditions like diabetes, alcoholism, or drug abuse, it is much more likely to be the result of emotional factors. Dr. Gabe Mirkin writes: "Depression and worry are the most common psychological causes of impotence. Very often impotence for medical reasons can *lead* to depression or worry, which greatly complicates the return to potency."

Dr. Mirkin adds: "An impotent man should see a doctor—but he should also realize that an erection is *not* a prerequisite for sexual satisfaction, either in a man or his female partner. A doctor or sex therapist can offer expert advice."

9

All in the Family

Being a real father to your children is one job that no
one else can ever do as well as you.
                                            John E. Crawford

Men need family life to stay alive! Studies consistently
show that married men live longer and healthier lives
than do single men. Friendships with both men and
women and involvement in churches and other groups
and associations are important, but close relationships
with family members are the life blood of a man's physical
and emotional health.

Most men recognize their families as their primary
source of comfort and well-being. Through his family of
origin—parents, brothers, and sisters—and later through
his wife and children, a man experiences companionship,
support, and intimacy. To be sure, job contacts with
coworkers provide a measure of this as well. But as we
have seen, such relationships are often hampered by
competition and other job pressures. So the family stands
out as the center of a man's emotional life.

The changing family

The traditional family is changing. Population researchers predict that more people will delay marriage in the future, and those who do marry are likely to postpone and limit childrearing to one or two children. In addition, more wives than ever before are deciding to juggle homemaking with outside employment. More distressing than these changes by themselves is the fact that more marriages are ending in divorce, creating more single parents, step-families, and weekend fathers.

No matter how it changes, however, the family will continue to be the main focus of a man's most important and meaningful relationships. As a result, men must be prepared to do some changing too. The man who is unable to find ways of adapting to today's family structures will be unable to gain the support and intimacy he needs.

One of the most important family skills a man can develop is the ability to work cooperatively in relationships built on equality and mutuality. Working together rather than ruling over and running over other family members is an approach that will go a long way toward building family unity. "Don't do what I do, do what I say" simply doesn't work anymore. We do not advocate the undermining of a father's authority with his children, but we are saying that authority needs to be used in more responsible and effective ways, ways that meet the unique needs of today's families. Unfortunately, many men still resist such changes.

The two-career family

Some men have difficulties adapting to a wife who works outside the home, especially when she is more successful than her husband. Actually, nearly six million American wives—about one of every eight in the nation—earned more than their husbands in 1982, making wives the primary income source for 12% of husband-wife households. Many men are threatened by a woman whose job success challenges their own. They may respond with jealousy and increased competition rather than pride and cooperation. This may explain why in one study, 60% of the wives had jobs outside the home, but only 30% of the husbands believed that their spouses should work. One man confirmed this attitude with a story about the first few years of his marriage:

When I first got married, it was extremely important to me that I make more money than my wife, which was very irrational because I was in the army at the time and we were poor. Joan was able to go out and work, but I do remember feeling threatened by her bringing home a good paycheck and me being stuck in the army. I don't think I broke out of that until I began to identify a career for myself. Once I got that, then I was able to let go, but when I was feeling directionless and stuck, it was very difficult for me.

Interestingly, no matter how large their paychecks, working wives are usually still held responsible for the majority of the housework. But more of today's men are now doing housework as well.

When men do take more responsibility for household jobs, many are faced with the dilemma that has long confronted working women: how to balance home interests with career demands, finding enough time in the day to accomplish all that needs to be done and still saving time for one's own personal needs and interests.

While some men have trouble adjusting to a wife who

works outside the home, others push their wives in that direction in order to increase the family income. When his wife decided she wanted to quit her job, Jack admits that he first felt miffed. "We had always been partners in making money, and if she stopped working it would put more financial pressure on me. I guess maybe I was a little envious of her ability to just quit working."

The second income generated by a wife who begins working outside the home can take some pressure off a man. Don, a dentist, said, "When my wife started teaching full-time, I no longer had to be the sole breadwinner. I was able to cut down on the hours I work, and now I have more time for other things I want to do."

If your wife is considering taking an outside job, or already has one, here are some things to think and talk about together:

1. *Count the cost.* Will the additional income and experience be worth the additional strains on the family? For some families, a second income is really needed; for others it is used only to increase the level of consumerism.

2. *Decide who will do the housework.* If your wife has been doing most of the household tasks and she is now going to add a 40-hour-a-week job to her schedule, obviously something will have to give. How much housework are you willing to do? How much can your children realistically do? Can you use some of the additional income to pay someone else to do some tasks?

3. *If you have children, plan how you will continue to meet their needs.* Don't assume, for example, that teenagers necessarily need you less than younger children. It may be very important for them to have a parent around when they need to talk. If both parents are work-

ing full-time, figure out ways to schedule quality time with the children.

4. Discuss problems and tensions as they arise (and they almost surely will). A husband, for example, may feel resentful because of the added pressure of child care or having more household tasks to do. A wife may feel that her husband is not doing enough. Before tensions build up, sit down and talk openly about how you feel. If the children are old enough, you may want to bring them into the discussion as well.

Fathers and children

While some men are willing to assume a greater share of the family responsibilities, especially when both parents are working, many still have problems with caring for their children, particularly preschool children. One father talked about the challenge this way:

To work out two careers is really confusing. In my family my mother did most of the parenting and disciplining. In Judy's family all that was shared by her mom and dad. We come from totally different poles, and we're trying to balance some place in the middle. We get into conflict just because of the different parents we had. She's more comfortable with our having two careers and her not caring for kids as much. I get in trouble because two careers are fine with me as long as she does all the parenting.

A dramatic study by Dr. Urie Bronfenbrenner, an authority on child development, addressed the degree of involvement on the part of fathers with their younger children and revealed some startling results. Bronfenbrenner put microphones on young children from middle-class families to determine the amount of time fathers spent with them in one-to-one play. He found the average daily time to be less than a minute! When the fathers were asked to estimate how much time they spent with their children, they rated themselves much higher, 15 to 20 minutes daily—quite a difference! While the amount of time fathers spend with children may increase as those children grow up, for many men it does not. Another study showed that most men spend more time shaving than they do with their children. No wonder that when kids were asked if they had to choose between their father and their TV set, most chose the TV!

When circumstances have forced men to become more involved with their children, the outcome is often very positive. Bill, who is a professional man now in his early 40s, discussed some of the changes in his family resulting from his wife's decision to enroll in a graduate school program.

The big challenge for us has been with Carol going to school full-time. Up until now, it's been pretty traditional, and I've been pretty lucky because I had the first pick on jobs. I have always seen my role as meshing with hers, to balance it. We used to ask each other, "What has to be done, and who's going to do it?" That's been changed now. "My whole schedule revolves around hers. I try to pay attention to the kids and their needs much more so now than before, emotionally too. The kids are starting to come to dad more, because mom is studying. It's really been good for us and for them too. Carol's frustrated sometimes because she feels she can't do everything she thinks she should. But when I was in school, I didn't do it all either. Now the roles are reversed, and I think she has to recognize that. I'm willing to do what I have to do to support her. It's exciting to me.

The lack of quality time between father and children can create serious problems. A father's physical or emotional absence from his children perpetuates the limited identity of father as "provider" and "worker" as well as absentee authority ("Just you wait till your father gets home!"), but does little to encourage a father in the role of friend. When children hear, "Don't bother your father, he's too busy…or too tired," both children and parent are deprived of needed intimacy.

Some of the distance between fathers and their children can be credited to the stress in a marriage relationship added by a new child. When a baby is born, a woman's needs for intimacy are met largely through her close contact with the new child. A man who is unable or unwilling to involve himself with the baby does not gain that same satisfaction. In addition, because sexual relations between husband and wife are often suspended for a time before and after the birth of a child, a man can feel frustrated, jealous, and left out. These feelings can breed resentment toward wife and child and further distance the father from contact with the baby.

When this pattern of noninvolvement begins early and is maintained during the child's formative years, it is not easy to change. "Distant" fathers tend to develop unrealistic expectations about what the child should be and how it should perform. They do not have realistic estimates of a child's capabilities. Such a father may become so critical and performance-oriented that he is never able to develop a warm caring relationship with his children.

Some fathers try to rationalize their lack of closeness with their young children by saying, "There really isn't a full person there to relate to. When he's older, I'll spend more time." But they may find that difficult to do when the proper groundwork has not been laid. In contrast, those men who are actively involved with their children from an early age on report stronger feelings for their children and greater involvement with them. It is this rationale that has led more physicians to encourage the inclusion of fathers in the labor and delivery rooms. It is estimated that 85% of expectant fathers are now present during labor, and up to half are in the delivery room at birth. Establishing a bond between father and child cannot begin too soon.

The single father

It should come as no surprise to most husbands how difficult it is to stay home with and have the major responsibility for the care of children. Their wives have been saying that for some time. But as is usually the case, you have to walk in another person's moccasins before you truly understand. More men than ever before are now in the position of having sole responsibility for raising their children, and they are finding that the job is not easy. Men who have suffered the death of a spouse are often required to take on the full responsibility of childrearing as well as household management. And in the case of divorce, more men are actively seeking and winning custody of their children.

Most single fathers have several important adjustments to make. Perhaps the most difficult is balancing the demands of a career with the responsibilities of full-time parenting. A man has to get involved with and get to know his children in a much more close and intimate way, a task that can prove quite difficult for a father who has previously not spent a great deal of time with them.

If he does not know how, a man has to learn to cook and clean. Finally, he also has to find a social life for himself. One man told how he received some unexpected encouragement in this area from his seven-year-old daughter. "We went out to dinner one night and were sitting at the table in the restaurant. Alone at the table next to us was a very attractive young woman. My daughter called out loud enough for all to hear, 'Now there's a nice woman for you, dad!' It was pretty embarrassing, but I could see that even at her age she realized that I needed someone for me too. It just made me feel that she understood a lot more than she seemed to."

Recent research by Dr. Kyle Pruett at Yale University indicates that fathers can be successful parents. He found that infants predominantly cared for by their fathers from birth were above average in the development of their social skills and that fathers were just as intensely loving and skillful as mothers.

Larry, a father who took over full care of his two children when the youngest was one year old and the oldest five, had this to say about his fathering experience:

Everyone said, "You can't do that. A man can't raise two kids, especially two girls." But I'm stubborn. There wasn't anyone who was going to stop me, and I was going to do everything two parents could do and more. I had to finally realize that wasn't going to be the case, but that was what I thought at first.

I don't really look at what I'm doing as a sacrifice, but I did have to compromise my life-style. I don't think there's any way around that. And it's been a real struggle from an income standpoint. I was used to working 40 to 50 to 60 hours a week on the road and then coming home with another 20 hours of paper work. All of a sudden you've got a house to take care of and two little kids to be with. Things have to change.

Sometimes I feel like I'm in the middle of a tunnel and I'll never get out. Before I was worried about one person and providing for three others. Now I'm worried about all aspects of three peoples' lives. That can get to you. But then you just say, "Hey, I'm going to do the best job that I can and then let things run their course." I feel like I've done a pretty good job getting them through the last seven years, and obviously they couldn't have done it without me—but I sure couldn't have done it without them. They've been as much of a support structure for me as I've been for them.

Fathers and sons

When the father-son relationship is positive and healthy, a father is a crucially important role model for a growing boy. His actions and attitudes transmit a way of relating and being in the world that is invaluable for the younger, "apprentice" male. A father who has close relationships with other men will model the ways that friendships can be established and maintained. By his actions both inside and outside the home, a man to a great extent determines how his son will relate to women and later, his own family. There is no better example for a boy than a father who loves and is involved with his family and who cares for and shows affection toward his wife.

Sometimes the father-son relationship includes strain and conflict. Some fathers become overinvolved with their sons, communicating expectations that are too demanding and unrealistic, causing alienation. Excessive competition can also develop between a father and son, usually with negative consequences for the son. Doing better, earning more, and making a greater contribution than one's father are common goals for sons in our success-oriented society. Such desires, however, can lead to great frustration for a young man whose father has always been highly successful. These sons often turn away from the heat of such competition, sometimes giving up completely on any effort to excel. Fathers can defuse this negative competition by not deliberately provoking or encouraging it. Allowing a son to choose his own way rather than deciding for him will also prove helpful.

An article in *Changing Times* magazine says, "Studies show that the 'heavy father,' who is distant and who punishes more than he rewards, increases the odds that his son will reject him as a model of what a man should be. Furthermore, the father who is very masculine in traditional ways outside the house but who never helps to make decisions or do what needs to be done at home does not influence his son very much at all."

Fathers and daughters

The father-daughter relationship is also highly significant. A girl who has experienced a positive relationship with her father is more likely to succeed in life. Several researchers have found that fathers of successful women nurtured their daughters' talent and made them feel loved, competent, and attractive at an early age. Women are more likely to be achievers if their fathers treat them as interesting people worthy of respect and encouragement.

Too often, fathers pass off responsibility for their daughters to their wives, with the excuse that a woman understands another woman better than a man can. Such a view is not only sexist, but shortsighted as well.

In many instances, the father-daughter relationship is more comfortable for a man than that of father-son. A man with three daughters commented, "I wouldn't have it any other way. I think if I had three sons, I would have botched the whole thing because I would have tried to make them be something I wanted them to be rather than let them be something they wanted to be."

Just as a man's first understanding of women comes through his relationship with his mother, a woman's comes through her contacts with her father. A close and effective relationship between father and daughter is beneficial because it gives a girl a healthy, positive view of men. Growing up with an emotionally absent father, a girl forms a distorted picture of men as aloof and nonresponsive. As a result, she may experience unsatisfactory relationships with men later in life. On the positive side, the father who takes time to develop a close bond with his daughter is helping her toward healthy relationships with men and later a successful marriage. And he is providing himself with more of the joy, intimacy, and pride that are the positive rewards of parenting.

On the road to being a better father

Because today's working life is often competitive and highly impersonal, truly intimate friendships rare, and neighborhood and community ties tenuous at best, it is through family relationships and daily family life that we receive the emotional experiences and fulfillment we need. This is clearly the most important task of the contemporary family.

Today's men need to see the family as their major asset and their best investment. It is through our children and their lives that we leave our most important mark in the world. If we were to work as hard at family life and childrearing as we do at our businesses, jobs, and careers, what a significant mark that would be and what a rich reward we would reap in terms of intimacy and personal satisfaction!

But how does a man work at improving his family life

and family relationships if he did not himself have a happy family experience? What if he grew up with parents who were neglectful or abusive? What does a man do if he did not have a father who modeled positive family involvement? Is he bound to repeat these destructive patterns? Is it possible to learn a new way?

In general, we tend either to repeat the patterns we grew up with or attempt to reverse those patterns, saying, "When I have kids I'm going to do things differently." This is because powerful but subtle influences are not easily overcome—especially if we are not consciously aware of them. When we become more sensitive to the pattern and style of our own parents, we may be on the way to making positive changes—but it will still be difficult if we have not had good models.

Some men who are trying to be better fathers purposely set aside time with their children, plan activities, and in general try to "make up for what I didn't have." This is not as easy as it might first seem. Without having experienced a close parent-child relationship, a man may find it difficult to relate to his own children. Tolerance and patience in working with children is learned by having been shown tolerance and patience as a child. In the process of learning how to be a better father a man is bound to make mistakes. He may find it hard to accept that his children would rather play with their friends then be with him when he is available. Then too, he runs the risk of becoming overinvolved with his children. In the case of a father and son, this often occurs in the area of sports. Or a father may try to control or hang on to a son or a daughter too long, with the likelihood of alienating them as a result.

On the positive side, many men have been able to learn from their own experience. By means of greater self-understanding and personal awareness we can change, but it is important to understand that change is rarely rapid, dramatic, or complete. But by combining some of the positive experiences of our own childhood with some freely chosen new ways, we can develop a unique family pattern that will give greater happiness to ourselves, our wives, and our children.

Here are some tips on increasing your degree of emotional and personal involvement with your family.

Open up more with family members. This means actually looking for times when you can share more about yourself and your daily life. Too often fathers become the questioners of other family members, listeners, and problem solvers, but don't come to their wives or children with their own hurts and successes. Family sharing and intimacy is a two-way street. Don't expect to get something if you don't give something. You have to be willing to risk.

Be careful about being quick to judge. As fathers, our first reaction to a problem is often to assign responsibility or to teach a lesson. One man, talking of his own childhood, said, "My father never fixed the problem; he always fixed the blame." If you want your children to talk to you, you have to be willing to listen and hear both the good and the bad and refrain from being excessively judgmental.

Keep the lines of communication open. If you have trouble speaking your thoughts directly, write down what you think and feel in a note or a card. Letters and other forms of written communication are the most treasured gifts that children and spouses can receive, especially from a father who is away or who may no longer live at home.

Robert, age 49, writes a weekly letter to family and friends. He started this practice 18 years ago when he was working overseas. Then it was a way of keeping in touch with relatives. As his children grew older and left home, he added them to the list of recipients. The weekly letter keeps them in touch with one another as well as with their parents. Every Tuesday morning he gets to work a half hour early and uses the time to "bang out" a newsy letter. He then sends copies to his three children who are away from home and to others he wants to keep in touch with.

If you find writing to be difficult, learn to touch more. An arm around your wife, a gentle hand on a son's shoulder, a playful hug for your daughter can say more about how you feel than the most eloquent speech.

Understand that your children are growing and changing. Your children are on their own life journey. You need to learn to accept their incompleteness and their own unique paths.

Be alert to getting caught in your own childhood traps. If your father had unrealistic expectations for you, you'll need to be careful in that area with your own children. If you were indulged and exempted from responsibility, you may not be very objective about responsibilities for your family. This is a particularly important area for today's families because of the large number of families where both parents are working full time.

Plan times and experiences together. These don't have to be two-week vacations to Disney World in order to be meaningful. Learn about the little things that your children like to do. Rather than always making room for them in your world, enter theirs. Play a game they choose rather than one you like. Better yet, let them teach you one you don't know, and watch them delight in your participation.

10

A Man and His Body

Our body is a machine for living. It is organized for that,
it is its nature.   *Leo Tolstoy*

When Tolstoy called our bodies "machines for living,"
he could not have anticipated how closely the American
male would come to translating his words into literal
truth.

One of the most striking paradoxes concerning men in
our society is the importance they attribute to physical
masculinity, bodily strength, and athletic ability, while at
the same time the degree of carelessness, lack of concern,
and even downright destructiveness they demonstrate in
the way they treat their bodies.

Men emphasize performance and ability, guts, and
staying power, whether they are talking about their jobs,
their sexual performance, or their recreation. Many men
try to prove their manliness by demonstrating:

- how strong they are
- how long they can go without rest

- how much they can eat or drink
- how often they can have sex
- how little they need help from others
- how far they can push themselves and their bodies

These men act as if their bodies are in fact machines, mechanical contrivances that require little attention and that will never wear out. Actually, many men give better care to their cars than to their bodies. Preventive maintenance of the body is seen as unnecessary at best and unmanly at worst. The focus is to keep driving, keep performing, keep producing—no matter what the cost.

And the cost can be great: premature aging, ulcers, alcohol addiction, drug abuse, sexual dysfunction, heart attacks. The list is long. All are stress-related conditions that invade bodies that are not machines, but uniquely constructed movable "temples" that require protection, consideration, and care.

New reasons for body care

Men have always had good reasons for taking care of their own bodies, but two recent changes now give men even more reason for paying closer attention to their physical well-being.

The majority of men's jobs no longer require or develop physical skills and abilities. Our modern service-oriented technological society does not make the same kind of physical demands on men as in an earlier era. From the time men roamed the earth in bands, hunting for food, until the Industrial Revolution, a man needed physical strength and agility if he was to be a successful provider. Today only a small part of the energy needed to run our society is provided by "muscle power."

For generations men have been developing labor-saving machines that enable them to get by with less exercise. Today we have to find ways to build that physical exercise back into our lives. For many, the only physical activity of the day is getting out of the car and walking to the desk or work station. If men today are to be physically fit, they will have to develop that fitness somewhere other than on the job.

Membership records at the YMCA show that the number of men over 30 who joined the Y has almost tripled in the last 20 years. Private health clubs are springing up all over the country. All of which suggests that more men (and women) are finding their way to fitness. Dr. Norman Shealy, a leading figure in the wellness movement, estimates that in 1979 only 5% of the adult population was concerned with diet and physical fitness. In 1984 he estimates that 20% of adults are making conscious decisions to improve their diet, exercise patterns, and general health.

A second reason why men today are more concerned with physical well-being is that *life expectancy is lengthening, and available leisure time increasing, requiring a longer period of activity and healthy physical functioning.* In a recent article the American Council on Science and Health quoted population statistics that suggest that "under ideal societal conditions the average age of death would be approximately 85 years of age." During the last 100 years, Americans have steadily approached that ideal. Men are living longer. If they are to be "fully alive" as long as they live, it will be necessary for them to care for the "temple" in which they live.

The best way to increase life expectancy and to improve the quality of life in the later years is to slow down the aging process—to delay or eliminate the symptoms of aging, such as heart attacks, hypertension, strokes, and arthritis. A man who is physically active, as well as interested and involved in life, can reduce or prevent the symptoms of old age and slow down the aging process. Men who are physically fit enhance their self-image, feel and act more mentally alert, and get more enjoyment out of life. At no point in their lives are men more conscious of their bodies than in middle adulthood. At this time many men must make a decision about changing the ways they have been living and how they have been treating their bodies.

Although it begins earlier, it is in the middle 30s and early 40s that a man becomes aware of the decline in his physical functioning. Along with a gradual but steady increase in body weight goes a corresponding reduction in physical strength, stamina, and reflex action. Many men also experience increased fatigue, worry over physical health, and depression.

The crisis of mid-life, reconciling one's dreams with reality, and facing the unavoidable evidence of increasing age and the limits of life, has to be resolved. When it is not, a man can experience further deterioration, depression, and a negative resignation toward life.

For a journeyman, however, the selection of a new way can lead to new life, exuberance, and renewal. This usually includes a new respect for one's body and a more deliberate effort to care for one's physical resources. A man can learn to pay attention to the cues his body provides, rather than shutting them out in the bullheaded denial of youth. He is able to see the wisdom in the old saying, "What you prevent needs no cure."

To help you think through the issues of physical self-care, we suggest seven basic principles.

1. Increase your level of physical activity.

Although the number of people in this country who exercise regularly is increasing, there are still too many men who agree with the old joke, "When I feel the urge to exercise, I lie down a while until the notion passes."

Physicians tell us that to maintain a healthy cardiovascular system we need to engage in exercise that approximately doubles our resting heartbeat for 15 minutes at least three times a week. This kind of regular, vigorous exercise strengthens the heart so it does not have to work as hard, and it increases one's lung capacity, thus improving oxygen supply and circulation. In addition to strengthening heart and lungs, a regular exercise program:

- improves muscle flexibility, prolonging an active life
- increases the range of motion for bones and joints
- creates and maintains muscle tone and firmness, improving appearance and strength
- slows down the aging process and potentially increases one's lifespan
- reduces stress and tension
- promotes self-esteem and self-worth by creating feelings of well-being
- combats obesity by burning up calories

Joe reports: "One of the best things I have done for myself in the past five years is to start running. When I do it regularly, I feel better, more alive. It also helps me write. When I'm working on something, I like to go out early in the morning and run three or four miles. It seems that the longer I run, the more ideas bubble up from inside. Instead of feeling exhausted, I feel energized."

If you want to begin an exercise program, the following tips may be helpful.

Take a personal fitness inventory. If you haven't been exercising regularly, check with your doctor before you proceed. Without a thorough medical examination first, vigorous exercise *could* be dangerous.

Decide whether you really want to begin a regular exercise program. If you're doing it only to please your wife or your doctor, you probably won't stay with it. It must be *your* decision.

Decide whether you wish to find a partner or go it alone. Working out with someone else can be fun and motivating. However, it may put you back into the competition bind. There are some advantages to going it alone, like fewer scheduling hassles and being able to proceed at your own pace. On the other hand, teaming up with a family member or friend may help you keep at it.

Find an activity that fits you. Pumping iron isn't for everyone. Neither is jogging or racquetball. Don't worry about the latest fad; it's likely to be replaced soon. Try to find something you enjoy enough to stay with. Something you can do regularly in your area's climate and an activity that doesn't require expensive equipment is probably a good choice.

Follow a schedule, but take your time. Try not to miss a workout. The secret of success is consistency. The idea is to get started and stay with it. Don't try to become an Olympic star in two weeks. You're in training for a lifetime. Start slow and steady, but be sure you schedule some regular time. Three times a week for 30-45 minutes is an accepted standard.

Keep track of what you do. Consider keeping some general fitness records on yourself. Establish some realistic monthly goals and chart your progress. This will help motivate you to continue your program.

2. *Maintain your proper weight.*

One way to calculate this is with the "Ideal Weight Formula" suggested by Dr. Keith Sehnert in *Stress/Unstress:*

106 plus 6 pounds for each inch above 60 inches equals _____

Example: Ron is 5′ 10″. His ideal weight would be 106 plus 60 equals 166. If you are 20 percent or more above your ideal weight, you should seriously consider getting your weight down and keeping it there. A few tips:

Get more exercise.   Nearly all attempts to lose weight and keep it off are doomed to failure unless you increase your exercise level. Regular vigorous activity will help you lose weight for several reasons. It burns up calories. It raises your body's basic metabolic rate, so you burn calories faster. It releases the tension that encourages you to do "nervous eating." It may act as an appetite suppressant.

Eat regular meals.   Don't skip meals, especially not breakfast. If you skip a meal you're liable to make up for it by "binging" later.

Choose a balanced diet.   Be sure to include the four basic food groups in your diet each day:

Fruit-Vegetables: 4 servings
Grain: 4 servings
Animal/Vegetable Protein: 2 servings
Milk/Dairy Products: 2 servings

Don't eat between meals, and especially avoid sweets and junk food.   If you do feel the need for something between meals, let it be a piece of fruit, like an apple.

Cut down on fats.   Although the debate on cholesterol continues, a 10-year research study by the federal government concluded that heart disease is directly linked to the level of cholesterol in the blood. Basil Rifkind, director of the study, says that the research "strongly indicates that the more you lower cholesterol and fat in your diet, the more you reduce your risk of heart disease. For most men this means eating more fish and chicken and less red meat. Also decrease your consumption of eggs, butter, and cheese.

If your will power is notoriously low, consider joining a weight-control group. Making a permanent change in eating habits is difficult for most people. You may find it easier as part of a group. In most communities there are groups like Overeaters Anonymous or clinics and local hospitals that will give you guidance and support.

Take a long look. Don't try to starve yourself down to your ideal weight in the shortest possible time. You'll probably give up or if you do succeed, yo-yo back up again soon. Think of making small changes that will last for a lifetime.

3. *If you smoke, stop!*

More and more Americans are heeding that advice. A recent study shows that only 28% of adults now smoke.

There are many men who smoke who would like to stop, but who find themselves caught in the grip of a habit that is not easy to break.

As is the case with all change, the most important first step is truthfully answering two important questions: Do you want to stop smoking? and, Are you ready to stop now? If your response to both of these questions is yes, you might want to consider the following:

If you plan to quit "cold turkey," try to do so in connection with one of the national Smoke Out campaigns, participating in an "I Quit" clinic in your area, or with some other kind of "buddy" plan. You'll find it easier to maintain your resolve if you can share the struggle with someone else. They will be able to help support you, and you can return the favor.

If you think a more gradual reduction or withdrawal from smoking would be better for you, set a deadline date for total abstinence from smoking as a way of not letting yourself off the hook. Then establish some specific goals for yourself—daily, weekly, and monthly. An excellent book that employs such a behavioral approach to stopping smoking is, *Break the Smoking Habit: A Behavioral Program for Giving Up Cigarettes*, by Ovide and Cynthia Pomerleau.

4. Avoid alcohol or use it sparingly.

Because we often develop "blind spots" in those areas where we are having difficulty, many men are not readily aware that drinking is a problem in their life.

A part of any health assessment should include a few questions about drinking. The following 10 questions are of the kind commonly employed to assess potential problems in the area of alcohol use.

1. Do you drink?
2. How much do you drink?
3. Have you ever wondered if you sometimes drink too much?
4. Do you ever drink more than you intend to?
5. Has there been any change in your tolerance to alcohol?
6. Has drinking ever caused any problems in your life?
7. Has a family member ever been concerned about your drinking?
8. Have you ever decided to quit drinking for a while or cut down on your drinking?

9. Have you ever felt guilty about your drinking?
10. Have you ever used sleeping pills, tranquilizers, or other drugs?

Answering yes to two or more of questions 3-10 suggests the possibility of a drinking problem. Further evaluation or professional consultation is recommended.

5. *Learn and practice the skill of relaxation.*

Millions of Americans are victims of "hurry-up disease," according to University of Southern California cardiologist Dr. Gershon Lesser. "People in a constant state of rush are in a chronic chemical state of emergency. They're experiencing a 'rush' of adrenalin that overtaxes the cardiovascular system, placing a life-threatening strain on the heart."

The cure, according to Dr. Lesser, is literally a change of heart:

- Rethinking priorities, even if that means postponing activities or delegating responsibilities.
- Planning activities with enough time so that hurrying is not necessary.
- Learning not to be intimidated by unfinished business.
- Developing the art of relaxation through music, walking, solitude, meditation, and physical exercise.

For learning relaxation techniques we especially recommend the book *Stress/Unstress* by Dr. Keith Sehnert.

6. *Avoid getting hooked on chemicals.*

Don't take tranquilizers, sleeping medications, headache pills, and other central-nervous system depressants, unless they are prescribed by your doctor. Free yourself from dependence on over-the-counter medicines such as antacids, laxatives, and cold remedies. Along the same lines, try to limit your intake of caffeine in the form of coffee or cola drinks.

7. *Be sure to see your doctor when you need to.*

Our bodies regularly give us messages, but many men have learned to disregard these signals. We've picked up other messages like, "Don't be a big baby" or "Tough it out!" We live with the image of John Wayne, who, after taking four slugs in the stomach, still rode tall in the saddle.

As a result we may keep going to work when we belong in bed. We keep up a heavy schedule when we should slow down. Or we ignore the signals that should send us to our family doctor. The result can be a heart attack, a long-term hospitalization, or a dragged-out life operating at an energy level far below our optimum.

What are some signs that you should stop "toughing it out" and head for the doctor? Dr. Keith Sehnert, M.D., author of a forthcoming book on self-care, suggests that these symptoms should not be long ignored:

- excessive daydreaming about getting away from it all
- increased use of alcohol, cigarettes, tranquilizers, or stimulants
- worry about trivial things
- a difficulty in making decisions, especially small ones
- sudden outbursts of temper
- sleep disorders

- stomach hyperacidity and pain
- heart palpitations and chest pains
- consistent headaches

By learning to listen again to these signals we stop treating our bodies like machines that keep running until they break down. Instead we can recover the biblical image of our bodies as the "temples of the Holy Spirit," gifts of God that deserve our best care.

11

Spiritual Growth for Men

I do believe; help me overcome my unbelief!
Mark 9:24

Two days after his graduation from high school Bob announced to his parents, "I'm going into the army." They thought that was a good place for someone inclined to get in trouble. In the army he became a paratrooper and was named "Soldier of the Year."

After his discharge he worked as a mechanic, soon owning his own garage, then several garages, then several fast-food places. He was working 16-17 hours a day, but the success seemed worth it.

At age 25 I was making 10 times more money than my father had ever earned. I kept buying bigger houses and more cars. Whenever I felt like it I flew to Canada for a fishing trip. I knew I was successful, yet something was wrong. No matter how good things were, it didn't seem to matter. I felt hollow inside.

I decided I needed something else in my life. We started going to a church in our neighborhood. One Sunday the pastor preached on John 10:10: "I have come that they may have life and have it more abundantly." After the service I said to the pastor, "You mean to tell me I'm going to find the abundant life in church?"

He said, "No, not at all. You'll find it in relationship with Christ."

Later we talked some more and I ended up on my knees asking Christ to take over my life. The hollow feeling went away, and it never came back."

Many men—especially in middle adulthood, after they have established themselves in a family and a career—experience that hollow feeling, that feeling of meaninglessness. They begin to ask, "What's it all about anyway?" They begin a search for spiritual growth.

Psychiatrist Carl Jung wrote: "Among all my patients in the second half of life—that is to say, over thirty-five—there has not been one whose problem in the last resort was not that of finding a religious outlook on life. It is safe to say that every one of them fell ill because he had lost that which the living religions of every age have given to their followers, and none of them has been really healed who did not regain his religious outlook."

For some men this may lead to a rather dramatic conversion experience. For others, especially those who have grown up in the church, it may be a more gradual awakening to the realities of their faith. Dan, a 52-year-old engineer, said, "I went to church every Sunday. Until I was 35 I heard the words, but they didn't have any meaning for me. Then in a series of evening meetings at church I gave myself to Christ. That led to a whole series of different choices."

Sometimes a crisis initiates this journey of faith. For Stan it was his divorce and the breakup of his family. For Ted it was his son's involvement with drugs, which led him into an Al-Anon group and the decision to turn his life over to a Higher Power. For others the beginning of the journey is so gradual that they don't even realize it's happening. But in one way or another, many men begin the search for meaning, the search for God, and at the end of that search realize that all along it was God who was searching for them.

Discovering God's place in one's life is not like a morning's hike or a weekend excursion. It is a journey that extends over a lifetime. There are indications that an increasing number of men (and women) are setting out on this most important of journeys. A July 1983 Gallup Poll revealed a substantial increase in the number of Americans who are attempting to "find God." For example, nearly two-thirds of the Protestants surveyed said they were more interested in religion now than they were five years ago. More than 50% indicated belief that religion can answer the problems of the world. The survey found that a surprising 26% of Americans, approximately 43 million people, are participating in Bible study groups, as compared with 15 years ago, when only 19% were involved.

Despite these positive indicators, many men continue to have difficulty committing themselves to a life of faith, perhaps because believing in God and living in a faithful relationship with God are inconsistent with a "masculine image," at least as our society defines it. According to this stereotype, "real men" aren't religious. Let's look more closely at some of the barriers men must surmount on their journey of faith.

Barriers to faith

1. Intellectual barriers

We men have been taught that before we make a decision we should "get the facts," "use your head," "think it through." We want things straight and clear. We say, "If God exists, let him prove it to me." In our scientific and technological age we have been taught to be logical rather than emotional. Like the disciple Thomas, we want physical proof before we believe. Yet like Thomas, we may need to hear Christ's words, "Blessed are those who have not seen and yet have believed" (John 20:29).

Thinking through the issues can be an important aid to faith. It may be important to you to find a group or class in which you can raise your questions and openly discuss your doubts. Missionary E. Stanley Jones wrote, "A faith that does not hold your mind will soon not hold your heart."

But faith is not merely an intellectual head trip. Elton Trueblood said, "Faith is not mere intellectual assent, but the supreme gamble in which we stake our lives upon a conviction. To believe that water will support our weight is one thing, but to trust our lives to it is another. The former is mere belief, but the latter is the commitment which is the heart of faith."

2. Emotional barriers

An active faith relationship with God requires us to open up emotionally. It means living in a way that puts us in close contact with our inner self. It requires an examination and confession of our most personal feelings. It means submitting to God, asking for forgiveness and forgiving others. While this attitude and behavior can help us reach our full potential as men, it can also be disturbing and threatening.

One of the biggest stumbling blocks in the development of a man's faith may be a fear of dependency. As we have seen, men are encouraged to "go it alone." "Stand on your own two feet," we're encouraged. "Be your own man." A man is expected to take charge of his own life, to make command decisions, and to take care of others. We have not been allowed to feel comfortable in anything other than an independent role; but such a role interferes with our relationship with God.

In writing about religious worship, John Reed refers to a condition he calls "extra dependence"—being reliant on a source greater than ourselves, outside ourselves, beyond ourselves. To experience the full spiritual and emotional benefits of worship, we must allow someone to minister to us. To do so, we must be capable, at least for a time, of becoming dependent.

Reed points out that many practices in the typical worship situation suggest submission and dependency: bowing the head, folding the hands, kneeling, confessing, receiving absolution, praying, receiving the sacrament, and receiving a blessing.

For a man who is afraid of being dependent, or who has trouble accepting his feelings and acknowledging his deficiencies, a close relationship with God may pose a serious threat to his manliness. Others may see such a relationship as a necessity. Abraham Lincoln said, "I have been driven many times to my knees, by the overwhelming conviction that I had nowhere else to go."

3. Psychological barriers

A man who trusts in God gives up a measure of control in his life. Having faith in God means following God's lead rather than our own, entrusting our life to God and to God's will. It involves coming to an awareness that God has a plan for my life, and it may be a very different course from the one I've chosen.

The control issue is central for many men. For most men the beaten path is characterized by control—control over one's self, over one's feelings, over other people. For men, control is power. So often, rather than submit to God, we want to control God—really, to be God. The following allegory illustrates this attitude:

A man hung precipitously over a yawning chasm, suspended only by a thin, fraying strand of rope. He struggled to climb upward and avoid a disastrous fall.

Seeing the desperate man in his plight, God spoke, in love, urging him to trust and let go of the rope so God might catch him.

Unsure as to whether he could believe that God would indeed catch him, and unwilling to relinquish his own control, meager as it was, the man refused to let go.

So he continued to hang there, able neither to climb higher nor to let go, his relationship with a saving God incomplete and his life hanging in the balance.

The problems of submission and control continue to be an issue for a man even after he has begun his spiritual journey. Men who have been taught to lead rather than follow and to compete rather than cooperate may have difficulty serving others through the church.

A close relationship with God requires some difficult adjustments for many men. It requires that they:

- open their lives to a higher power whose existence cannot be objectively established
- make a commitment of the will and the emotions as well as an intellectual commitment
- let go, give up, and give in rather than control
- experience a sense of dependency
- serve others rather than dominate and rule over them

The power of the gospel

The good news of the Christian faith is that God is a loving parent—a Father who accepts us and loves us with an unlimited and unfailing love. Out of love God identified with us and entered our history in the person of Jesus Christ. If we want to know what God is like, we have only to look to Jesus. The *gospel*—the good news—is that God is like Jesus—accepting, forgiving, caring. Because we know that God loves and accepts us, we can love and accept ourselves as we are.

Jesus was more than a good man and a great teacher. At the cross he offered his life to set us free from our past and present mistakes and shortcomings. He asks us to follow him and he offers us a new kind of life. He sends his Spirit into our lives to guide and strengthen us. Because of Jesus' liberating power, we can now say with St. Paul, "Forgetting what is behind and straining toward what is ahead, I press on toward the goal to win the prize for which God has called me heavenward in Christ Jesus" (Phil. 3:14).

When we turn and trust God's goodness and grace, when we "let go of the rope" and allow God to free us from the things that enslave us and to give us new life, we experience an inner peace that renews and refreshes our minds, bodies, and spirits. No longer do we have to control and take care of everything. We know that God is in charge of the universe and that we can turn to God for help.

Jesus the man

In his life on earth, Jesus provided us with a practical model for living a new life. This model is particularly helpful for today's men as we look for new directions, meaning, and role models.

Jesus broke the traditional male role of his time. In many of the ways we have already identified, he was a journeyman. He was both a carpenter and a teacher, at home with physical work as well as reading the Scriptures and teaching in the synagogue.

Jesus was a caring, nurturing man who experienced love, compassion, anger, and sorrow. He had feelings and was not ashamed to let the them show.

He was able to care for others, nurturing and healing the sick, but he was also able to accept care, allowing a woman to bathe his feet and dry them with her hair.

He was capable of relating to all kinds of people, old and young, children and wise men, male and female, Pharisees and sinners.

Jesus was independent, yet he sought out the company of others. He chose disciples and loved them as friends and helpers.

He was committed to his ministry—even to the point of helping others on the sabbath—but he also knew how to relax and how to have fun. He attended a wedding where he provided the wine. His enemies accused him of being a glutton and a drunk. Yet he was a disciplined servant of God who often went off by himself to pray.

Jesus did not seek material gain or political power, yet he is the most influential man in history.

It was some of these qualities that inspired one man to say, "In Jesus I see the picture of the kind of man I ought to be." If that seems to be an unattainable goal, we need only take heart in the words of Bernard of Clairvaux, "What we love we will grow to resemble."

Some directions for the spiritual journey

1. Don't try to go it alone. The spiritual life is not for the Lone Ranger. Join a church. Get into a Bible class or prayer group. In many areas there are groups especially for men. If there isn't one, you may be instrumental in getting one started. Get involved with others who are seeking God's will for their lives. A wise Christian leader gave this advice: "If you want a close relationship with God, find some people who have it and be with them."

2. Build some time in your day—even 10 or 15 minutes—for spiritual growth. Use it to read the Bible or other inspirational literature. Take time to pray.

This means, to begin with, that we need to schedule time to be alone, preferably in a quiet place. Henri Nouwen writes, "Without solitude it is virtually impossible to live a spiritual life. Solitude begins with a time and a place for God, and him alone. If we really believe not only that God exists but also that he is actively present in our lives—healing, teaching, and guiding—we need to set aside a time and space to give him our undivided attention."

Most mornings Ron gets up an hour earlier than his wife and children. He makes a pot of coffee and then begins his day with devotional reading. Sometimes it is a favorite part of the Bible, like the Psalms or one of the Gospels. At other times it is a spiritual classic or a contemporary guide. The best kind of devotional reading leads directly into prayer. With his thoughts focused on God he is ready to wake the family and help get the children off to school.

Matt, a young businessman, said, "I don't have any trouble feeling close to God when everything's going great and I can say, 'Praise the Lord.' And, strangely enough, I feel close to God when I've got my back to the wall and I say, 'God, help!' At times like that he always comes through. But where I tend to get lost is in that gray middle area of daily life."

A daily period of solitude can help us keep our bearings in the midst of the busy-ness of our crowded lives. We can use the time to communicate with God about our priorities and problems and concerns. And through spiritual reading we can open our lives to the transforming power of God's Spirit.

3. *Begin a journal.* A journal or day book is a place to focus your life. In it you can reflect on how your life is going, set new directions, and keep yourself headed in the direction you've chosen. It can be used to record insights gained from your reading, and it's a good place to keep a record of inspiring quotations you come across. Combined with Bible study, reading, and prayer, it can help you hear God's directions for your life. For specific directions on journal keeping, see *How to Keep a Spiritual Journal* by Ronald Klug.

4. *Consider a yearly or semiannual retreat.* Sometimes you may need to get away for a longer period of time to gain some perspective on your life and regain energy and direction. In many areas of the country there are retreat houses that are open to you—no matter where you are on the religious spectrum. Lacking that, you can

use a cabin, a motel, or even a tent. Take a weekend or several days in some place apart from your usual surroundings. Use the time just to be quiet, to rest, to rethink your life direction, to do some spiritual reading, to pray, to seek new strength and guidance from God.

12

Mapping Your Personal Journey

When a man's fight begins with himself, he is worth
something.   *Robert Browning*

At this point you may be saying, "Sure, I see the need
for some changes in my life, but I don't know how to start.
Besides, how can I make myself different? How does a
person change?"

The following exercise should help you identify an area
or the areas you may want to begin with. While none of
us knows ourselves completely, we can develop greater
awareness of what we need to work on. After you've com-
pleted the exercise, we'll talk more about the process of
change.

Mapping your journey

Think about your life as it is now. In each of the areas
shown, indicate how far you are down that path by
circling a number. Circling the number 1 would mean

you are an inexperienced traveler in that area, at the beginning of your journey. Circling the number 10 would mean you are an accomplished traveler, one who knows the area well and who feels little conflict or discomfort on that path.

After you have circled a number for each of the eight paths, think about how you would like your life to be. Go back and place an X over the number in each of the areas to show where you would like to be six months from now. How far along each path would you like to move in the months ahead?

Your Journey Map

Feelings	1	2	3	4	5	6	7	8	9	10
Friendships	1	2	3	4	5	6	7	8	9	10
Family	1	2	3	4	5	6	7	8	9	10
Male/female relationships	1	2	3	4	5	6	7	8	9	10
Work	1	2	3	4	5	6	7	8	9	10
Physical well-being	1	2	3	4	5	6	7	8	9	10
Leisure time	1	2	3	4	5	6	7	8	9	10
Spiritual growth	1	2	3	4	5	6	7	8	9	10

Now underline those areas in which you have circled the lowest numbers and those areas that contain the greatest discrepancy between where you are now and where you would like to be. These are good starting points.

Generally speaking, the areas in which your circles and Xs are within a number or two or are on the same number are areas in which you have some degree of satisfaction with your self and your journey. However, if you have circled a low number (3 or under), and have indicated your satisfaction with that progress by placing an X either on the same number or close by, you may find yourself at odds with others around you concerning your attitudes and behavior.

After reviewing the lists, you should be ready to choose an area to work on. We all have many areas of our lives in which growth and change would be beneficial. Some things are more difficult to change than others. Change doesn't usually just happen to us without our cooperation, so it is important to choose an area in which you have decided that you really want to change, rather than an area chosen by someone else.

Setting priorities

Many men today are already overloaded with *oughts*. We find ourselves saying, "I ought to lose 20 pounds." "I ought to get more exercise." "I ought to quit smoking." "I ought to spend more time with the family." "I ought to be more involved at church." And on and on.

If this book does nothing more than load you down with more oughts, it will probably do you little good. Some *oughts* are helpful. They can challenge us and point us in the direction of desirable growth and change. But too many oughts can make us so weighed down by guilt that we give up before we start.

We need to be able to choose a few realistic goals and then understand more about *how* we change.

The previous section, "Mapping Your Journey," has helped you identify some areas of your life that you may want to work on. Next you need to set some stepping-stone goals that will move you forward in your chosen area.

Take a piece of paper and at the top write the name of the area you're planning to work on: example—family life. Then think of five or six concrete actions you could take that would help you improve in this area. You may want to reread the related chapter.

Some possible goals under "Family Life" might be:

- Try to spend some time alone with each child every day.
- Go out for breakfast with my wife every Saturday so we can talk without being interrupted.
- Sit down with the kids and work out a plan for dividing up some of the household and yard tasks.
- Get the whole family involved in planning next year's vacation.

Try to keep your goals realistic. If we choose too many goals or choose goals beyond our potential, we are tempted to give up and resign ourselves to our old ways. It is far better to think in terms of small steps. When these have been achieved, we can move on with confidence.

The process of change may be slow. Deep-set patterns are not altered overnight. But every step forward—even the painful ones—will pay off in greater confidence, satisfaction, and happiness.

A friend recently gave this advice: "If you want to get started on jogging, don't set out to run 10 miles the first day. If you don't have a heart attack, you will probably be so sore that you will vow never to run again. For the first week, just put on your running shoes every day and take them off again. But do it every day. The next week put on your running shoes each day and walk once around the block. The next week, walk around the block twice each day. Then the fourth week start a little jogging." Amusing advice maybe—but realistic, and we can apply it to many areas of life.

How do we change?

Personal change is almost always a process, rarely a one-time event. Instead of a sudden dramatic transformation, we usually make small changes in our attitudes or behavior. Even when we hear of someone who changed "overnight," if we look closely we will usually be able to trace the beginnings of that change back to a much earlier time.

To be meaningful and lasting, personal change must take place on three levels: the thought level, the action level, and the feeling level.

Although the process of change can begin on any one of these levels, it must eventually result in some change of all three if it is to be effective.

Changing thinking

First of all, if we wish to be different, we do well to begin with changing how we think.

All of us struggle to some degree with negative thinking. We tell ourselves thoughts and ideas that limit our ability to feel and think positively and to function effectively. Psychologists call this *negative self-talk*. They maintain that our feelings are not caused by our circumstances, past or present. Instead, our feelings and our actions are the result of what we tell ourselves about our circumstances. Much of this inner thinking or self-talk is *irrational*—that is, it is characterized by distortions and misbeliefs, and thus can be upsetting and destructive.

Some of the typical misbeliefs or negative self-talk that men engage in include the following:

- "I can't cry; they would think I am weak."
- "If I don't push myself to the limit and get to the top, I won't be acceptable to others (or to myself)."

- "If I feel affection for a male friend, then I must be gay."

One way to change our thinking is to begin to identify and then challenge our negative self-talk and replace it with more rational, realistic talk. Thinking about the examples in the previous paragraph, we might counter with:

- "There's nothing wrong with showing feelings. Just because a man may cry when it is appropriate doesn't mean that he's weak."
- "I don't have to perform all-out every minute in order to be accepted by others. Even if I did, there are more important things than the acceptance of others—like my own health, well-being, and family relationships."
- "If I feel affection for another man, it means I'm alive! It's good to have positive feelings for others, and affection doesn't mean that I'm sexually attracted."

Another way to begin to change the way we think is to employ a process psychologists call "reframing"—seeing a problem, event, or experience through another perspective (seeing the glass half full rather than half empty, for example). Some people call this *positive thinking.* Descartes said, "I think; therefore I *am.*" Positive thinkers say, "I think; therefore I *can.*" One psychiatrist says he never allows his patients to discuss "problems." When the word is mentioned, he corrects the person and renames these "situations." Another positive-thinking journeyman who works successfully and innovatively in city government is known for his identification of problems as "opportunities for learning."

When we are able to reframe our thoughts and perceptions and see ourselves and our situations in a more positive, problem-solving manner (rather than with a pessimistic, defeatist attitude), we go a long way toward developing an ability to cope effectively.

Changing behavior

While altering our thinking is often an important first step toward change, there are also many instances in which we must change how we act. We must begin to translate our "reframed" thought into appropriate action. The old adage, "Actions speak louder than words," makes a great deal of sense.

For example, if we need to become more physically active, and we spend our time *only in thinking* about an exercise program but never doing anything about starting one, our physical condition will not improve. On the other hand, if we push ourselves a little to actually begin the process of exercising, often we can break out of some of our avoidance and negative thinking and experience some immediate reward, like the good feeling that goes along with doing something healthful just for ourselves. Although we may have to struggle against our old habits (and our aching muscles!) for awhile, after a surprisingly short time we discover that we have established a new pattern of behavior with many benefits. Moreover, these benefits then help us continue the new behavior we have begun.

Especially when our behavior is harmful to ourselves or to others (for example, excessive drinking), stopping that behavior has to be the first priority. Once the behavior has been halted, even temporarily, we can go to work on the feeling and thinking that may be perpetuating the behavior. While sheer will power alone will often not be enough to permanently correct the situation, when applied as a first step, it allows the development of other kinds of coping skills that together can help us permanently alter our behavior.

Changing feelings

Changing how we feel may be one of the most difficult changes we have to make. Feelings are often mixed, and finding the ways in which our feelings connect with the way we think and the way we act is not always easy.

An initial step in managing our feelings is to *own* them. This means becoming aware that what we feel is *ours*. We should not suppress or deny feelings, nor should we blame someone else for how we feel. Recall the "I messages" from Chapter 4 ("I'm feeling angry" rather than "You make me mad"). When we can accept the feeling as our own, we have a chance to change it. Remember: we never directly change someone else. We change ourselves, and others around us change in response to that change.

A second important step in changing feelings is *labeling* them. Labeling feelings helps us identify the kind of feelings we are experiencing. Surprisingly, we often don't know what we are feeling. How many times have you identified yourself merely as feeling "upset"? What does that really mean? angry? hurt? afraid? We have to learn to be specific about what we're feeling. When we label our feelings, we take them out of the realm of the mysterious and the uncontrollable. We can get a handle on them and begin to do something about them.

A third step is to *say how we feel*. Putting our feelings into words rather than suppressing them or impulsively acting on them is another important way we can learn to change how we feel. When we can say how we feel, we do two things: (1) we communicate more openly and honestly; (2) by saying how we feel, we discharge some of the intensity of our inner reactions, thereby reducing tension and stress.

Now that you have some idea of the areas in which change can be initiated, review your personal journey map and the areas in which you want to begin to make some changes. Identify the level (thoughts, actions, feelings) where it would be best for you to begin. For example, if you are concerned about a pattern of work addiction and you begin at the *thinking level*, ask yourself, "What kind of negative self-talk or distorted thinking is contributing to this behavior?" Are you telling yourself something like, "If I don't give 110% all the time, I won't be acceptable to others"? If so, begin to work at correcting this misbelief.

If your initial efforts were focused on some change in your *behavior* and your problem is work addiction, could you begin to reschedule your priorities? Would learning time-management techniques help? Can you begin to plan some vacation time? If you can't take a vacation right now, how about a regular exercise program that might combat some of the tension of overwork?

Finally, at the *feeling level* it may be helpful to identify some of the feelings you have about your job, what you think is expected of you, and the amount of time you work. For example, are you feeling depressed and unhappy with some other part of your life, and are you working excessively to deny or escape from your depression? Or are you afraid of failure, and thus feel you have to work more than anyone else to ensure success?

To really make progress in the area you've chosen, you'll have to work at all three levels. But you have to start somewhere, and once you do, change at any of the three levels will make complete change more possible.

Positive and negative strategies

When we attempt to manage problems, adjust to circumstances and demand, or make changes in our lives, we are employing *coping strategies*. These strategies can be either *positive* or *negative*. Most people who live successful and effective lives are not just lucky. They have learned to use coping strategies that are healthy and positive.

Positive strategies promote growth and competence in the person who uses them. They attempt to deal with the problem, confront the life issues involved, and figure out a solution.

Negative strategies tend to impede growth and reduce competence. They often avoid problems or handle them in ways that do not lead to effective solutions.

Why would anyone use a negative strategy rather than a positive one? This happens because at first both work. Both provide some immediate relief from the pain of the moment. In fact, the negative strategies are easier and thus more attractive because they require less psychological effort. Avoidance is almost always easier than confrontation. In the short run, negative strategies often work. Over the long haul, however, they tend to break down.

Examples of negative strategies

1. Avoid the problem. "Maybe it will go away." That's what we tell ourselves when we employ this strategy. But problems rarely go away. Instead, when we *avoid* we just *delay* and often *complicate* the problem. While it does provide temporary relief, avoidance usually creates *more* worry and tension, while doing nothing in moving toward an effective solution.

2. Deny the problem. This can be even more troublesome than avoidance. Denying is not just running away from a recognized problem; it is saying, "There is no problem." This head-in-the-sand approach buys time, but at a high price. Excess tension and a vague sense that things are not right are sure signs of too much denial.

3. *Cover up the problem.* Don't try to cover up the problem with another problem or symptom, like drinking, overeating, or working extra hours in an attempt to dodge the problem. These strategies work temporarily to delay the consequences of the problem, but they camouflage the real issue. The "cure" may be worse than the problem, especially if we fall into habitual drinking, overeating, or drug abuse.

Some examples of positive strategies

1. *Think about the problem.* Take a personal inventory in the area in which you are interested in making some change. What are your assests in that area? What are some of the liabilities holding you back? Consider reviewing your inventory with someone you respect and trust.

2. *Talk about it.* Find someone with whom you can express your feelings, what you are up against. That someone might be a good friend, your wife, a trusted family member, your pastor, or a professional counselor.

3. *Read about it.* Maybe you need more information. Once you have identified a problem area, do some reading to see what others have said or done. Each chapter in this book suggests some places to start.

4. *Try to figure it out.* Ask yourself the following questions:

- Why is this a problem for me?
- What is it that I'm doing (or not doing) that prevents me from further growth or change in this area?

- What am I telling myself about this that may be negative?
- What are my feelings about this problem?
- What three things can I begin to do that will move me forward in this area?
- Who can I call on for help if I need it?

Strength to change

The apostle Paul spoke for all men when he said, "I have the desire to do what is good, but I cannot carry it out. For what I do is not the good I want to do; no, the evil I do not want to do—this I keep on doing" (Rom. 7:19). Even with the best of intentions, we're left wondering, Where do I get the power to change? Making any kind of change is often difficult—and we need all the help we can get. Fortunately for us, God himself is ready to supply that help.

Henri Nouwen writes, "We live in a worry-filled world. We find ourselves occupied and preoccupied with many things, while at the same time feeling bored, resentful, depressed, and very lonely. In the midst of this world the Son of God, Jesus Christ, appears and offers us new life, the life of the Spirit of God."

Knowing that God loves and forgives us, we can love and forgive ourselves. This sets us free from a crushing sense of guilt and despair. It opens the way out of our loneliness, despair, and alienation. We are drawn outward to be more *connected*—connected with our selves, our bodies, our families, the earth, other people, and with God.

Through spiritual disciplines like those mentioned in Chapter 11, we open ourselves to the transforming power of God's Spirit. Bible study, worship, prayer, reading, time spent with other Christians—all these are the means by which God's power is released in us to produce new life.

When you need help from others

Despite our best efforts, sometimes we are unable to make significant life changes. Then we need to turn to others for help. This can be a difficult decision for men. It may be hard to admit that you need help, but it can be the first step toward personal growth and change.

Some men are finding help and support in fellowship groups with other men. By sharing their thoughts, convictions, and feelings with other men in a small-group setting, many men are discovering they are not alone in their struggles and concerns.

Such groups vary in style and procedure, but they are usually "leaderless" in the sense that they are not directed by any one person. Responsibility for some minimal direction, opening and closing the meeting, and serving as timekeeper is usually rotated. In this way the group's effectiveness becomes everyone's responsibility. Some additional suggestions for forming a men's group can be found following this chapter.

At certain times, individual therapy or personal counseling is a strategy that can provide focus and direction as well as impetus for change. There are many different approaches to counseling, but all try to get at the three levels we have discussed—thinking, behavior, and feeling. Sometimes a particular counselor will focus on one of these; for example, cognitive therapy concentrates on thinking; behavioral therapy on actions; psychodynamic therapy on feelings and experiences.

Whatever the approach, therapy is not something done *for* you or *to* you. It is something you do for yourself with the help and direction of an experienced guide. It is a way of learning about yourself and the patterns in your life that create problems. And it is a way of learning how to change those patterns.

If you think you might benefit from personal counseling, you can locate a counselor by talking to your pastor, a school guidance counselor, your physician, or the professional psychologists' association for your state.

Embarking on the journey

Finally, we recognize that whatever we discover about ourselves, our problems, and our lives is incomplete and fragmentary. What is important is to be willing to make the journey. For it is in the quest, not the accomplishment, that a man finds dignity and worth. We embark on the journey, called forth by God's Spirit. On this most important journey of all, God is our empowering presence, our source of meaning, and our ultimate goal.

Lord, God, I turn my life over to you.
I believe that you love and accept me as I am.
I let go of my past with its failures, unmet obligations, and unfulfilled dreams.
For the sake of Jesus Christ, forgive me and set me on the journey to new life.
Lead me to the people I need and those who need me.
Give me a vision of the man I might be.
Help me make wise choices and set realistic goals.
Strengthen me for this life and lead me to life eternal.

Suggestions for Starting a Men's Support Group

1. Find one or two other men whom you think might have some interest in the idea. Invite them to lunch to discuss it.

2. If this core group shows an interest, ask each man present to invite one other man to a similar luncheon or meeting next week.

3. At the second meeting discuss some of the potential benefits of meeting together on a regular basis:

- fellowship with other men
- a chance to learn how other men view themselves, their problems, and their world
- personal support for one another

4. If a minimum of three or more men are interested in beginning, meet together a third time to plan:

- a time when all can meet
- length of the meeting (usually 1½ to 2 hours)
- frequency of meeting (usually weekly or once every two weeks)
- a time commitment if you wish (10 weeks, 15 weeks, open-ended)
- a place for meeting
- a plan for the meeting (structured vs. unstructured, leader vs. leaderless, study and discussion, discussion only)

5. At the first "official" meeting agree to the confidentiality of the group so that all will feel comfortable talking openly and frankly. Then spend time going around the group and allowing each man to talk some about himself and his life as a way of beginning.

6. Many similar groups adopt the following format:

- one-third time for prayer or personal reflection
- one-third for study, the Bible, some spiritual reading, or self-help books
- one-third time for discussion

Questions for Discussion

Although reading this book can be beneficial in itself, we have found that discussing the book and the issues it raises in a men's group greatly multiplies the benefits. The following discussion questions are suggested to help you grapple with important issues for men. Even more important, they open the way for men to talk to one another about their problems and questions and to get to know one another.

1 Caught in the Middle

1. Do you know any men whose stories are similar to those at the beginning of this chapter?

2. With which of the interrelated problems on page 14 do you struggle most? Which do you feel you are handling satisfactorily?

3. How has our society changed in ways that call for a new kind of man?

4. In your view what are the problems most men in our society are wrestling with?

5. What do you hope to get out of reading and discussing this book?

6. If you have not already taken the test at the end of this chapter, do so now. How did you feel about the test? Did it give you any insights into yourself?

2   A Boy Becomes a Man

1. Where did you spend your boyhood years (to age 12)?

2. In what ways was your boyhood similar to Jerry Lindberg's? How was it different?

3. What did you learn from your father—by words or example—about what it means to be a man?

4. In what ways are you a "chip off the old block"? How are you different from your father?

5. What messages about masculinity did you get from your mother?

6. Which of the traditionally "masculine" traits on page 24 do you think are valuable and therefore worth retaining? Which tend to be destructive?

7. Can a man have some of the traditionally "feminine" traits and still be masculine? Can you think of some men who manage this balance?

8. Do you know some men who fit the description of a journeyman?

3   The Journey Inward

1. What is the journey inward? Why do some men have difficulty embarking on this journey?

2. Do you agree with the descriptions of the "beaten path" and the "less-traveled road"?

3. Discuss each of the polarities (like "competition

—cooperation"). Can you think of illustrations of these polarities in your own life?

4. Discuss the self-test on page 38. Do you sometimes follow one path at work and another at home or in another setting? Why?

5. In what areas of life do you feel the greatest need to control what happens? Where do you feel it easier to "let go and let be"?

4 Men Have Feelings Too

1. "Most men have learned to suppress and deny their emotions." Do you agree? How true has that been for you?

2. Can you think of situations in which your feelings are mixed or in conflict?

3. What is the difference between *suppression* and *repression* of feelings?

4. In what ways can unexpressed feelings be a problem? Which of these might be a problem for you?

5. Are you better able to express your feelings now than you were 10 years ago? What helped you make this change?

6. Which of the suggestions in the section "How to Express Feelings" are most important for you to put into practice?

7. Share the results of completing the "Assessing Your Feelings" exercise.

5 Friend and Brother

1. When you were a boy, did you have a special friend or group of friends? Do you still maintain any of these friendships?

2. Do you agree with the statement: "In boyhood most

men enjoyed a number of close friendships. As adults, however, most men find themselves without friendships that are satisfying and sustaining"?

3. What do each of these Bible verses say about friendship: Prov. 17:17; Eccles. 4:10; 2 Sam. 1:26; John 15:13-15?

4. Which of the barriers to friendship seem most formidable for you?

5. If you are to reach out in friendship to other men, which steps on pages 55-58 will be most important for you?

6. Have you ever had, or do you now have, a friendship with a woman other than your wife? What do you think of Alan Loy McGinnis' six ideas for managing a friendship with a member of the opposite sex?

7. If you haven't already done so, complete the "Roster of Fellow Travelers" and "My Friendship Response." In your group, share your reaction to these self-tests.

6 *Work: Frustration or Fulfillment*

1. Do you know anyone like Harold, whose story is told at the beginning of this chapter?

2. In what ways does your work give your life meaning?

3. Does your work create a strain on your family life?

4. Do you find close personal relationships at work?

5. If you're upset about something at work, what do you usually do?

6. Have you ever faced the trauma of unemployment? How did you cope with it?

7. When you finish your work day, how do you usually feel?

8. If you are retired, how have you adjusted to retirement? If you are not retired, what are you doing to prepare for retirement?

- Enter the average number of hours you spend on the following:

  Work (including business travel, work brought home) _____
  Family (meals, conversation, leisure, work together) _____
  Self (hobbies, reading, friendships, etc.) _____
  Community (church, volunteer, others) _____
  Rest (sleep, naps) _____

- Which of these activities get the largest percentage of your time? the smallest? Is that the way you want it? If not, what can you do about it?

9. How have you been influenced by the changing job picture?

10. Have you experienced any difficulty in working with assertive or aggressive women? How have you learned to handle such situations?

11. Which of the suggestions for low-stress working do you now follow? Which ones do you want to put into action?

7 Learning to Play Again

1. What are your favorite leisure-time activities?

2. Are there any ways in which you abuse or "waste" your leisure time?

3. How important in your life is watching, reading about, or discussing professional sports?

4. Do you find yourself to be so competitive or driven in your leisure that you don't enjoy it?

5. In what ways could you gain more enjoyment or benefits from your leisure activities?

6. What changes do you want to make in your leisure in the next six months?

7. Which of the ideas for low-stress living do you already follow? Which might be important for you to put into effect?

8 *The Women in Your Life*

1. How does your marriage or other male-female relationship compare with the story of Carl and Lois?

2. How would you answer the question, "Who is boss?" in that relationship? How do you handle disagreements or differences?

3. Describe your relationship with your mother. How has it influenced your relationship to other women?

4. How do you feel about your sexual relationship? Are there any changes you would like to make in that relationship?

9 *All in the Family*

1. What changes do you see happening in families? How is your present family different from your family of origin?

2. Has your wife worked outside the home during your marriage? How did that affect your family? What adjustments had to be made?

3. What kind of household tasks do you regularly perform?

4. If you have children, how would you describe your relationship with them?

5. If you are a single father, what are your major problems? How do you handle each one?

6. How was your relationship with your father? If you have a son, how is your relationship with him similar or different?

7. If you have a daughter, how do you relate to her? Is it different from the way you relate to a son?

8. What could you do to be a better father? What are you willing to do?

10 A Man and His Body

1. Are there any ways in which you treat your body like a machine?

2. What reasons do you have for taking better care of your body?

3. How would you describe your general fitness and level of physical activity? If you need more physical exercise, how could you get it?

4. What is your ideal weight? How does your actual weight compare? Do you have a plan for losing weight?

5. If you smoke, have you considered quitting? What might help you do that?

6. How would you describe your use of alcohol?

7. What are your favorite ways of relaxing? What steps could you take toward a more relaxed life-style?

8. Do you tend to abuse any chemicals or over-the-counter medications?

9. What is your attitude toward seeing your doctor?

11 Spiritual Growth for Men

1. How would you define "spiritual growth"?

2. Where are you right now on your spiritual journey? Where have you been? Where are you going?

3. Which of the barriers to faith have the greatest effect on you?

4. What gets in the way of your trusting God more fully?

5. With whom can you talk about your spiritual questions and problems?

6. In what ways is Jesus a model for your life?

7. Which of the "Directions for the Spiritual Journey" are you currently following? Which could you follow?

12 Mapping Your Personal Journey

1. If you haven't already done so, do the "Journey Map" exercise on page 132. In your group share the results of the exercise.

2. Choose the area you want to work on first. List some possible goals in that area. Decide which you will work on first. Share this in your group.

3. Discuss how we can change our thinking, our behavior, and our feelings.

4. What are negative and positive coping strategies? Can you think of examples from your own life?

5. Have you ever tried to make major changes in your life? What helped you change?

6. Under what conditions would you seek a counselor? How would you find one?

7. How can this group help you change?

For Further Reading

For individuals or groups who want to explore further the issues raised in *New Life for Men*, we recommend the following books:

Burns, David. *Feeling Good: The New Mood Therapy*. New York: Institute for Rational-Emotive Therapy, 1980. This book shows how by changing the way you think you can alter your moods, deal with emotional problems, and handle depression.

Conway, Jim. *Men in Mid-Life Crisis*. Elgin, Ill.: David C. Cook, 1978. Written from a Christian perspective, this book helps men understand the mid-life crisis and cope with it.

Foster, Richard. *The Celebration of Discipline: Paths to Spiritual Growth*. San Francisco: Harper and Row, 1978. A Quaker writer helps us regain the value and benefits of spiritual disciplines.

Greiff, Barrie S., M.D., and Preston K. Munter, M.D. *Trade-offs: Executive, Family and Organizational Life*. New York: New American Library, 1980. Writing especially for executives, two doctors offer strategies and techniques for managing a career and personal life.

Klug, Ronald. *How to Keep a Spiritual Journal*. Nashville: Thomas Nelson, 1982. A practical guide to keeping a journal for spiritual and personal growth.

Kuntzleman, Charles T. *Maximum Personal Energy*. Emmaus, Pa.: Rodale Press, 1981. A YMCA exercise consultant shows how you can "unleash your energy potential and eɪ.joy life."

Lakein, Alan. *How to Get Control of Your Time and Your Life*. New York: New American Library, 1974. One of the best books on goal-setting and time management.

McGinnis, Alan Loy. *The Friendship Factor*. Minneapolis: Augsburg, 1979. A best-selling book that gives sound advice for maintaining friendships with both men and women.

Sehnert, Keith W., M.D. *Stress/Unstress*. Minneapolis: Augsburg, 1981. A Christian physician provides a practical guide for understanding and managing stress.

Sheehy, Gail. *Passages: Predictable Crises of Adult Life*. New York: Bantam, 1977. A best-selling summary of the research into the stages nearly all adults pass through.

Tubesing, Donald A. and Nancy Loving Tubesing. *The Caring Question*. Minneapolis: Augsburg, 1983. Down-to-earth advice on striking a balance between self-care and care for others.